FREEDOM
IN CHRIST

FREEDOM IN CHRIST

An Introduction to Political Theology

PAUL LAKELAND

New York
Fordham University Press
1986

Printed in the United States of America

FOR
MY COLLEAGUES IN THE
DEPARTMENT OF RELIGIOUS STUDIES
AT
FAIRFIELD UNIVERSITY

Contents

Preface
to the Second Edition

There are very many books around at the present day on the closely related subjects of political and liberation theology, as anyone can easily discover who turns to the Bibliographical Appendix to this volume. There is, consequently, a need to explain why another such book, and one which is clearly so brief that it cannot hope to present the full complexity of the phenomena with anything like the exhaustiveness to which many weightier books pretend.

This book is intended for the fabled "general reader," that is, for someone who takes his or her Christianity seriously, and is truly interested in what is happening in the Christian Church but who could not argue that he or she continually keeps a finger on the pulse of contemporary theological development. For those who do keep abreast of theological advances, it may be that they will find little new here, although indeed the suggestions made in the slightly more technical second chapter may be of interest even to them. But for the rest, I hope it may serve to introduce them to something new, as well as relate that something new to the ancient wisdom of the Catholic theological tradition.

Freedom in Christ is an introduction to a complex phenomenon, or set of phenomena, which represents the most exciting development in Christianity today, and therefore deserves consideration. If I may be permitted to generalize a little: in the last twenty years the Latin American Church has gone from being a conservative body, whose pastoral activity was never allowed to threaten the political and economic status quo, to a network of communities, supported by the hierarchy, in which ordinary people express the vitality of their Christian faith by bringing the light of the gospel to bear upon the social problems of their own local context. "Liberation theology" is the name for the theology which has grown out of reflection on the recent history of the Christian churches in Latin America, and which to some extent also inspires those churches to move further.

As a theological direction, liberation theology falls within a small group of theologies which together can be called political theology. However different it may be from the others in the group—and in some ways it is quite different—it shares with them the conviction that serious theology not only must have a political concern, but must in some sense begin from the everyday experience of a particular Christian community. In this respect it can be associated with German political theology, with North American black theology, and with feminist theology in at least some of its forms. In fact, liberation theology has influenced all these movements to a greater or lesser degree in recent years.

This present book, however, is not just a description of the growth of liberation theology in Latin America. Indeed, it says little at all about Latin America. It is rather an attempt to explain the underlying theology of liberation theology, and to ease the reader toward the recognition of two issues: firstly, that even this form of political theology can be related to some traditional theological symbols, especially that of incarnation; and secondly, that a first-world Church such as our own simply has to face the challenge of liberation theology, both to our possible role as oppressors, and to our resistance to the incorporation of such a perspective into the life of our own Christian community.

For this American revision of the original British edition (1984), I have made a number of changes. In the first place, I have revised the entire text so that it addresses the context of this society rather than that of my former home. Secondly, I have greatly enlarged the Appendix, to make it into a kind of reader's guide, recognizing that if this book serves its purpose, it should stimulate readers to pursue some one direction or other in greater depth. Thirdly, I have added an extra chapter on Vatican attitudes to political and liberation theology, an issue which has really come to a head only during the last year. I hope that all these changes will make the work more valuable.

Finally, I have to thank a number of people. The book's dedication expresses my indebtedness to my colleagues in the religious studies department at Fairfield University, simply for providing a congenial working environment, a blend of freedom and collegiality that one would have to go far to match. I am also grateful to the

English Jesuit journal, *The Month,* and to its editor, Mr. Hugh Kay, for permission to use material that first appeared in the pages of that excellent journal. I should also like to thank Gerard P. O'Sullivan, then of Fordham University Press, who first suggested the idea of an American edition; Walter Petry, for first-hand information about the Latin American background; and Beth Palmer, my wife, for patiently suffering my need to meet yet another deadline.

Fairfield University
July 1985

1

The Nature of the Beast

ONE OF THE MORE PAINFUL EXERCISES I can recall from English lessons in my schooldays was poring over poetry in search of "figures of speech," which we were then required to classify. The classifications seemed always to be according to incomprehensible Greek terms. I remember that Milton's *Paradise Lost* was a favorite mine for the figures, one of which was the phrase "darkness visible." This was held up as an example of the "oxymoron," an apparent contradiction of the noun by its accompanying adjective. The peculiarity of this figure, we were told, was that despite the contradiction it seemed to cling to meaning, and in some mysterious way even to intensify it.

To some, "political theology" may seem to be another prime example of an oxymoron. The adjective is taken by many to be a contradiction of the noun: "Politics and religion do not mix. . . . The Church should keep its nose out of politics. . . ." But might not this phrase too survive the paradox and achieve new insights?

The currently disreputable state of politics and the political life is a partial explanation of the unwillingness to talk of "political" theology. Over a hundred years ago, Disraeli could say that politics was frequently wrongly defined as "the art of governing mankind by deceiving them." In the late twentieth century we may be forgiven for thinking that government and deception are not always total strangers. If we call someone a "politician," we may be intending to imply that he or she is indifferent to the means necessary to obtain what is desired. "Politicking" means wheeler-dealing. Moreover, to say that something makes "sound political sense" or that it is a matter of "political expediency" is usually to imply a contrast with

1

what is the more ethical or "idealistic" course of action. It is, then, no surprise that many people argue for the independence of theology from at least this kind of politics.

Even if we recognize that behind the suspicion of politics and politicians that exists today there is a positive and worthwhile meaning to the words, it may still be hard to see what they have to do with theology. Politics is usually referred to as the science or art of governing society. Nothing could be more thoroughly "secular." Its object is the ordering of our everyday world of national and international relations, and the acquisition and defense of prosperity and security. The various departments of the state are the means to this end. Politics deals only with the temporal welfare of the inhabitants of country or even world, and it does not interfere, it is often said, with the individual's freedom of worship. Is it not true, in fact, that democratic political societies respect the independence of Church from state, and grant freedom of religion to all citizens? And is it not equally the case that at least the Christian churches respect the autonomy of the state in the organization and regulation of secular affairs? "Render to Caesar the things that are Caesar's, and to God the things that are God's."

Even if we understand politics as positively as possible, therefore, it seems as if political theology might lead to just such dangers to democracy as occur when the Church interferes in areas in which it is said to have no business. Most nations, of whatever political complexion, are familiar with the charge that the Church is "meddling in politics." Of course, the unspoken assumptions behind such accusations are intensely problematic, and the total separation of ecclesiastical and secular powers may itself be one of those assumptions.

From another point of view, the term "political theology" may be held to imply a distortion of theology rather than an interference in the natural autonomy of the political. Traditionally, theology has been understood, in Christianity, as the study of God's revelation through Jesus Christ. It has concerned itself, for reasons which we need not go into for the moment, with the relations of God and the individual. A presentation of the core of the gospel so understood might run something like this: "Jesus Christ, the Son of God, came into the world to save sinners, and in following the message and example of his life and teaching, and in believing that he is indeed true God and true man, the individual Christian can come to salvation. A life lived in this faith, in communion with other believers under the teaching authority of the Church, will lead to a life with God."

The traditional formulation of faith I have illustrated above has something to recommend it. Its emphasis, however, is on the individual, and on the preparation of the individual here and now for the reward of salvation in the life to come. It is all too easy to caricature, pick holes in, and ridicule any position, and this is no exception, but while respecting it, its inadequacies have to be pointed out.

The traditional viewpoint almost totally excludes any idea that everyday matters, including the political and the domestic, have any value in *themselves* for the Christian life. Of course, the traditional theologian would not deny the importance of the Church community, or of the conduct of Christians toward one another and toward all human beings. But the significance of these acts and matters rests not in the acts and matters themselves, but in the way in which they sustain or prepare the individuals for the eventual reward of their personal, individual faithfulness to God.

The belief that politics has its place—the secular world—and that religion has its place—the individual's faith and the praying and believing community of the Church—is a neat compartmentalization of functions that reduces if it does not eliminate confrontation. It is a view shared by all Communist governments, by most if not all of the Latin American military dictatorships, by the Constitution of the United States, and by most citizens of western European nations. The boundaries of state and Church activity may be differently drawn in different societies, and the penalties for crossing them may be more or less severe, but they exist almost everywhere. And on the face of it, as we have seen, there is considerable justification for such "separation of powers."

The very name of political theology is a rejection of the views outlined above. Political theology argues that there can be a fruitful union and a happy marriage between two admittedly unwilling and uncomfortable bedfellows. It disagrees with the notion of politics I have illustrated, and with the ideas of God, religion, and salvation we have touched on. Consequently, it does not adhere to the separation of powers of religion and politics. It is therefore not surprising that few religious leaders and no world heads of state subscribe to it. Moreover, it does not consider itself a compartment of theology, like "moral" or "dogmatic"; instead, it sees itself as the whole of theology, or as a whole way of doing theology. At its simplest, it believes that living the Christian life in the world *is* salvation. But this needs amplification.

In the first place, political theology does not accept the definition of politics as the science of governing or ordering society, but treats it rather as the activity of building society. In other words, it does not look upon political activity as the work of the leaders of the country, but as the concern of the whole people. To some extent, this reflects the fact that the origin of vigorous political theology is in the less-developed and less-democratic societies of what we know as the third world—in particular, of Latin America. In such societies, by and large, the building of a just and democratic society by the people is of necessity contrasted to the governing and ordering of the existing unjust and repressive system by the politicians. A favorite accusation against the Church's work in such societies is to label it "subversive," but this frequently means simply that the unjust status quo is threatened by an alternative vision of society.

4

We may naturally and perhaps rightly protest at the suggestion that this is where we too stand, in our own relatively democratic societies. Certainly, the more democratic the society, the more complex the problems of practicing a political theology. Our priorities for society, as Christians, may not always conflict with those of our genuinely if only partially representative governments. Moreover, the complexity of almost all sociopolitical issues may incline us to leave them to the politicians, and restrict our involvement to a vote every four or five years. But, the "political" in political theology aside for the moment, we are concerned with political *theology*. That is to say, we are dealing with our way of looking at God and God's relationship to the world, and in that matter we have no choice but to have an opinion and make a commitment. *Political* theology simply defines the dimensions of the arena in which we expect our theology to function, and the mode of our activity within that arena. If we took "political theology" as a partial discipline, we might be able to describe it as something like "the theology of the governance and ordering of society," and there is no doubt that as Christians we could have some pointed and constructive remarks to make about it. But, as we have said above, political theology is an integral way of looking at the whole of life. We are forced, then, to follow the third-world understanding of political activity as building rather than governing society. That is to say, the political in political theology directs us to the whole of human secular existence as the arena for theology. We said earlier that the fundamental belief of political theology is that living the Christian life in the everyday world *is* salvation. We can now fill this out.

Political theology argues that theology is found, understood, put into practice, and validated within human secular existence. This may seem a somewhat shocking statement to make, reducing Christian belief and practice to day-to-day existence, a "secularization" of the Christian tradition. I hope we

5

can show that this is not so, and an important preliminary for that is to recognize that theology has a qualified importance.

Theology is not what religion is for, and is not identical with religion. The vast majority of religious people get along perfectly well without theology, and there are quite a number of theologians who apparently manage without too much overt religion. But theology is an attempt to understand and interpret the revelation of God. Just as psychology would not exist without the human psyche, and there would be no economics if we did not trade with one another, so there would be no theology if human beings did not respond to God speaking to them in the world. Religion is a term for the human response to the revelation of God. And theology is its servant, not its master. It tries to understand the revelation and the response. And its objects are therefore God, human beings, and the relationship between the two.

The only implication of the preceding argument which we need emphasize for the moment is that the nature of God, and consequently the nature of God's relationship to human beings, is revealed and appreciated only in human life. Whether we seek that revelation in reflection on the Bible, in the following of Christ, in prayer and contemplation, or in our daily lives, they are all activities which take place in the everyday world, and they are all somehow creations or acts of human beings. This is what it means to claim that our theology is found, understood, put into practice, and validated within human secular existence. Political theology has something to say about all four stages, and about the order in which they occur.

To say that theology is *found* in the world is not just to claim that doing theology is a human activity, which of course it is, or that there is a place where theology exists to be discovered—in the Bible or in papal teachings, for example—and that we can uncover it there. Rather, it is the claim that the material out of which theology is made is the everyday experience of ordinary human beings. Theology, as we have already

6

said, is a form of reflection, and the experience has to be there for us to reflect on it. What *political* adds to this is the belief that positive, concrete human actions directed toward the construction of a better world are particularly significant material upon which to reflect.

The second stage is that of *understanding*, born out of the relationship of theory and practice. Obviously, reflection on experience does not have to produce theology; it could equally well result in a religiously neutral philosophy, or mere head-scratching. A Christian theology is the result of interaction between an individual or community and the Christian revelation. Theology is therefore a process of reflection on experience, taking place in the mind of an individual or in a community which stands within a particular religious tradition—in our case, the Judaeo-Christian tradition. Understanding occurs when we relate our experience to our tradition, and so create our own way of looking at things.

We said that theology is *put into practice* in the world. But what we are putting into practice, we can now see, is a way of understanding derived originally from the confrontation between the gospel and our everyday experience. Consequently, when we put it into practice, we shall not necessarily find ourselves doing something differently, or adopting new courses of action, although we may. But we shall certainly find that the theology brings a new coherence to our vision of Christianity, and makes sense in terms of the Christian revelation of what may already seem quite clear in terms of human solidarity. Christians have always striven to practice what they preach, but sometimes it may be necessary to preach what is practiced.

Finally, we said that theology is *validated* in human existence. Sometimes, we may incline to think that an intellectual exercise, which theology undoubtedly is, is self-validating. We look on it as a sort of game, which makes sense on its own terms as long as the participants follow the rules. And, truthfully, much theology has been constructed and carried on in

7

such a way. But political theology is different; there is a stage, that of understanding, which is an intellectual exercise, but the validation does not occur at that time. The theology is valid if, put into practice as a deeper understanding of human life, it results in or leads to right action—practice that is truly directed toward building up the community.

These four stages will recur again and again in our treatment of political theology in the course of this book. Taken as a whole, they underline the fact that political theology is a new departure in theology. Like traditional theology, it is concerned with God's revelation in history, but unlike much traditional theology it stresses God's action in revealing. God truly acts in the world, speaking to human beings through action; hearing the word of God, therefore, is achieved through putting oneself in union or solidarity with the activity of God in the world. As we shall see in the next chapter, God's activity in the world is found in human action, first of Jesus Christ, then of all human beings. Consequently, God's activity in the world is not superimposed upon human history, as if an occasional earthquake or famine were the divine comment on our poor human efforts; rather, the interpretation of human life in the light of the gospel sets the believers on a path in which God's purpose is at least partially apparent.

Political theology is also fundamentally Christian theology. Obviously, the kind of association between divine intent and sociopolitical activity demands a very close relationship between God and humankind. It is in Jesus Christ that God has established the relationship with which we are invited to be in solidarity. The possibility of human action's being interpreted with any justification as divine activity lies in God's speaking the word that it *is* so. Jesus Christ is that word. This is what it means to have a christocentric religion; the word communicates God's purpose, but also God's being, and the Christian God is therefore Jesus-shaped. The problem is that the shape of Jesus can be perceived very differently, as we examine the scriptures and our traditions, according as the various images strike upon this or that imagination, for our imaginations are modified by our upbringing and experience.

We have so far considered two preliminary definitions of political theology. We began by saying that "living the Christian life in the everyday world *is* salvation." We then amplified that: "Our theology is found, understood, put into practice, and validated within human secular existence." A third definition can now be added to this, one which I am borrowing from the writings of Dorothee Soelle, a leading German political theologian. Political theology, she says, is a "hermeneutic, which . . . holds open an horizon of interpretation in which politics is understood as the comprehensive and decisive sphere in which Christian truth should become praxis."[1] Political theology, in other words, is an understanding of reality in which Christian faith is tested by the quality of the involvement of believers in building a just and free society. It is very single-minded, as you can see. No doubt, the complexities of Christian doctrine remain, and theological wranglings may persist, but it is only in the concrete conditions of the *polis*, of human secular and socio-economic activity, that they have any significance. The test of sound belief will be the quality of the life of the believer, and that life must be politicized.

We can now return to the question of secularization. In this initial discussion of political theology, we have tried to see why and how a theology can take the human world as its context. In the next chapter, we shall look more deeply into this, and into why it does not necessarily entail a reduction of Christianity in the world. For now, however, and for the remainder of this chapter, we must try to see if it is right to look on political theology as a form of secularization, and to ask, if so, in what way this might be considered a positive development.

Secularization can simply mean the reduction of all that has to do with God, Christ, and religion to purely human matters. Then, Jesus is seen merely as a good man and great teacher, and his life-work as the preaching of moral perfection. His resurrection becomes only the memory of him which remained among his early followers. He is placed as a prophet alongside Buddha, Ghandi, Marx. He becomes a Great Thinker or Great Maker of the Western World, and may even get his face on wall-posters and tee-shirts. His words and deeds, paradoxically, are prized with a kind of literalism and ahistoricalness which is also the mark of extreme fundamentalism. The significance of existence is exhausted in the value of his teachings.

The problem with the crudely secularizing interpretation of Christ is that it involves moving substantially away from the memory of him in tradition. As a result, it becomes a supremely arbitrary interpretation. That is to say, when we leave the tradition behind, more often than not we find ourselves relating those portions of the tradition which attract us to bits of modern knowledge or opinion which, with our late twentieth-century minds, we hold to with a fierce and irrational conviction. The nineteenth-century liberal Jesus is replaced by the flaxen-haired, all-American SuperJesus of biblical comics, or the hippy Jesus, or Che Guevara with a halo. Any such approach reduces the gospel by interpreting it solely according to the presuppositions and prejudices of some particular historical moment. The method of political and especially liberation theology is strikingly similar and subtly different. For the platitudes of the hour it substitutes the hard-won convictions of a life with the oppressed. In place of the abstract, theoretical theologization of the Christ, it hears the gospel confirming the struggle for liberation. It is inductive, not deductive.

There are two further senses of secularization on which we must touch. The first we have inherited from the tradition of the Reformers, above all from Luther. Its starting-point is with the belief that between God and human beings there is an absolute qualitative distinction. It owes a great deal to a particular interpretation of Paul's Letter to the Romans, and begins from a view of human beings as radically sinful. Since the Fall, human beings have been helpless sinners, and they are restored to God's favor through the divine justification of the individual as, through faith in Jesus Christ, they are saved.

From the Reformers' perspective, faith has principally to do with the relationship of the individual to God's justifying grace. Relations between individuals in the everyday world, the moral sphere, have nothing *per se* to do with faith. They therefore have nothing of themselves to do with salvation. If salvation is by faith alone, then ethical rectitude has no part in it. At the same time, strangely enough, the impact of this view in history has been to stress moral uprightness, perhaps as an escape from a total privatization of salvation in unassailable subjective conviction. If salvation is given to some and not to all, then there has to be something distinctive in the lives of those chosen by which the community can recognize the saints. But carried to extremes, perhaps as seen in Bunyan's *Life and Death of Mr. Badman*, it can begin to look as if sound business practice and a conventional life are marks of God's favor.

There is no doubt that this Reformers' model establishes a kind of autonomy for secular existence. God does not interfere in the world of works, because it is of no importance to God in the final analysis. Human history, even the pursuit of goodness and truth, has nothing to do with salvation, and thus secularization here means the emancipation of the world from divine interference. Such a view has had positive benefits for the twentieth century, particularly in the ethical sphere, as exclusively religious judgments on moral questions have been subordinated to the conviction of the informed adult conscience. The world "come of age" is supposed to go on according to its own internal rationale, and establish its own order of priorities. Working for the political utopia will have no connection with the coming kingdom of God.

Among the advantages which this view of secularization

ought to bring with it is that it should carry those who accept it away from the temptation to read revelation as a series of rules and regulations about moral conduct in this earthly life. It ought to establish a sense of the total human responsibility for our actions and our world. It should promote human solidarity. Above all, it should encourage Christians not to capitulate too quickly to negative forces in the world under some mistaken understanding that what happens must be "the will of God."

Unfortunately, the results of the Reformers' model for secularization are not necessarily so positive. Although humans are freed to be responsible upon their own strength in the kingdom of this world, they are also deprived at the same time of their motivation—at least when times get hard. Human solidarity is only ever a problem when it is personally disadvantageous, and unless a human being can find an absolute demand for selfless solidarity with the rest of the human race, all that remains to fall back upon is sheer stoicism, a barren call to duty, or a woolly-headed humanism.

The relationship that human beings have with their God is the basis of what they take to be of absolute importance in their lives, but secularization as the emancipation of the world suggests that either everyday existence has no real importance at all or God has become irrelevant to life. The relationship with God is not on the side of the world at all. The world cannot therefore have absolute significance. As a result, political activity will be understood as the process of safeguarding the rights of individuals within a state in relation to one another and to the state, and the rights of nations against one another. Politics will remain at the level of governing society, not of building it up, not least because the individualism of this world-view, which is a direct result of its divorce from God, leads to a concentration on the inviolability of the person. The collective, whether the state or the world community, is an object of suspicion.

It is no surprise that the areas of the world which we associate with Protestantism—Western Europe and North America—are the homes of the great liberal democracies which represent this model in practice. And it would be foolish to suggest that these societies do not have much to commend them. Citizens of these states have considerable individual freedom, and their rights are well safeguarded. It is, though, evident to almost anyone that it is in these countries that religious indifference has become most widespread, perhaps because the total emancipation of the secular leads to the establishment of an alternative secular salvation in which success and affluence not only cushion the more fortunate pilgrims through the vale of tears, but even sometimes become representative of righteousness.

The political price of this model, as we have already said, is that politics is understood merely as governing society. There is no room for a concept of politics as the people building its own society. Moreover, the relative freedom of the liberal democracies and capitalist societies in their internal organization may from some parts of the world appear to translate into an outwardly dictatorial mien toward the less powerful or wealthy nations. That is to say, the emphasis on the preservation of the rights of the individual and the safeguarding of the rights of the nation over against other nations takes precedence over concern for the moral health of the community or the demands of international justice. No concept of human solidarity can find a place in such a scenario, and no reasonable argument can be maintained for paying attention to the rights of others, if they seem to infringe the rights of self—whether that self is individual or "my" country. At its most extreme, capitalism creates a completely free society with no checks on individual freedom. All may carry guns, and the weakest go to the wall.

This is not a simple condemnation of advanced capitalism, but a warning of what happens to society when its political life discards its commitment to the absoluteness of the human. Christian incarnational anthropology is one form of such views of the human. The emphasis on *citizens'* rights rather than *human* rights seems to follow from discarding the incarnational perspective in favor of the absolute qualitative distinction between divine and human. This latter offers no provision for community morality; all that even the Church could demand would be an *expectation* that the believer would deal justly with his or her neighbor. And the history of the West in the nineteenth and twentieth centuries bears eloquent witness to that being wishful thinking.

The so-called incarnational perspective is the final sense of secularization which we must consider. We will approach it in detail in the next chapter. It is the core of political theology and of the Catholic tradition in Christianity, although it is neither the exclusive possession of Catholics nor universally held by them. Briefly, instead of arguing that God's justifying grace, received in faith, establishes a "religious" relationship between God and the individual, thus freeing the everyday world for its own secular path, this view calls attention to the incarnation. The incarnation is the actual union of human and divine in Jesus Christ. As a result of this event, the way is open for Christians to see their own activity in the world as God's action in history. The incarnation is also God's gift of self to human beings, demonstrating God's love for humans for their own sake. The incarnation is thus the revelation of the value God places upon the world. The world is of intrinsic worth, and human actions have the potential for being the mediation of God to the world. Indeed, on this view it is hard to see how else God could be mediated to the world. Consequently, human beings can see themselves as charged with the responsibility for mediating God's love of the human, and so transforming the world into a more human and loving response to the self-gift of God.

The implications of the incarnational view for political activity could not be further from those of the previous model. Now we discover at the centre of religion not the distant God touching the individual with justifying grace, but the incarnate God expressing absolute love of and faith in the human race. The human community, not merely the individual, is made out to be of absolute significance. Political activity, like all other human actions, is marked and changed by the divine revaluation of the human. Politics has to serve the human community, rather than the individual or the state. True political activity becomes corporate human action aimed at building up the human community. What in our world we are accustomed to call 'politics' is a lesser matter, servant of the other, justified solely by the extent to which it supports the community's self-realization.

For the moment, we shall go no further into this model, since the relations of politics and incarnation are the subject of the next chapter. Let us in conclusion simply recall our definition of political theology as "an understanding of reality in which Christian faith is tested by the quality of the involvement of believers in building a just and free society." In the definition the emphasis is on the primacy of practice, whereas lately we have been stressing the theological basis of integrated religio-sociopolitical activity. This oscillation between theory and practice will be a feature of this book, as it is a feature of political theology. The one cannot manage without the other, but if we have to choose, then we should remember that the one who will enter the kingdom is not the one who calls "Lord, Lord," but the one who does the will of God. Even, perhaps, if that one is not aware that it is the will of God which he or she is striving for.

NOTE

1. *Political Theology* (Philadelphia: Fortress, 1974), p. 59.

2

Politics and the Incarnation

I WANT TO BEGIN THIS CHAPTER by inviting a comparison between two quite similar experiences with which I would wager
most people are reasonably familiar. The first of them is the
sense of awe which occasionally suffuses a person confronted
with some towering human achievement. The second is that
experience of wonder which is so frequently a concomitant of
the appreciation of natural phenomena.

At one time or another, I would imagine, we have all
stood before something which spoke to us of the heights to
which human beings can attain. My own sharpest such experience took place in Salisbury Cathedral Close on a quiet sum-
mer evening, but the places and things which speak to me in
this way are limited by my cultural conditioning and background. Others may share some or all of them, or differ vi-
olently. I have no doubt that there will be almost as many
choices as there are people to make them, and this does not
matter in the least. What is crucial is that the experience must
have evoked wonder at the *human* achievement displayed there-
in. We must all unearth our own examples from our private
histories.

It seems equally likely that most of us can also recall moments of wonder at the beauty or grandeur of great natural
phenomena. Very many poets, artists, and philosophers, particularly those of a more romantic disposition, have celebrated
this experience. Their choices, and our own, seem to cluster
in a surprisingly unimaginative fashion around mountains,
oceans, sunsets, tornadoes, and waterfalls. This is not important and should not be disconcerting. Each experience is unique,

and agreement on what occasioned it is evidence only that human beings are made very much the same.

Responses to these experiences of natural beauty fall into two categories. Some people do not move beyond their wonder at the scale or the poignancy of the beauty before them. Others, consciously or not, move on to some sense of the createdness or contingency of the beauty, some apprehension of its dependence on something other than or beyond itself. The second group, in other words, sees it as God's work, because they believe in some kind of creator God, although in practice it does not seem that the quality of the experience differs all that much from one group to the other.

Experiences of wonder at human achievement, our first group, display similar divisions. Some people will experience no need to move beyond their sense of the genius of human beings, while others will fashion a kind of link between the human creation of beauty and the divine creator. Once again, the difference will not necessarily be in the quality of the experience but in the associated network of views about the world.

The constitution of the groups in the parallel sets of experiences is not, however, identical. In the case of the experience of natural beauty only the theists will be able to proceed to a sense of the creator's role, and all the theists will presumably be moved to do so. However, not all theists will take the same step in the contemplation of human achievement. We can of course put all unbelievers in the category of those who will simply marvel at human creativity, but they must rather surprisingly be accompanied by those Christians who favor the absolute qualitative distinction between divine and human. If the relation between God and the Christian is restricted to the realm of God's justifying faith, and if the world is the world of works, then human creativity in the world comes into the category of autonomous secular activity—autonomous not only in the sense that human beings are responsible for it, but also in the sense that it is ultimately of no importance to God. Consequently, human creativity is divorced from divine creativity, and the experience of natural beauty and the experience of the products of human genius will fall into different orders of experience.

The incarnational perspective holds the two sorts of experience together. On the one hand, it adheres to a belief in the creator God who is to be worshiped among other reasons for the beauty of the world. But the incarnational anthropology which forges that close link between human and divine implies that human creativity is an important dimension of the human role of acting as agents of the divine in the world. This human creativity also occurs in a world which, because it is of incalculable importance to God, is the arena of the sacred for human beings.

We have just argued that atheists and some Protestant Christians share an attitude to human achievement, the one because they do not believe in a creator God, the other because the creator God they believe in plays no part in day-to-day human activity. However, the two groups will be divided on the importance they ascribe to human creativity. The unbeliever will be inclined to talk about the *absolute* value of the human being, and therefore about the ultimacy of human achievement and creativity, whether it is the production of a painting or the creation of a socialist republic. But the Christian will in fact ascribe absolute value to God and thus completely *relativize* all human achievement. The incarnationalist, on the other hand, as a believer in God, will not subscribe to the absolute value of human beings, but as a believer in the unity of the divine and human activity, he or she cannot entirely relativize human beings. Incarnationalists will therefore speak of the *intrinsic* value of human beings.

Behind the labels of absolute, relative, and intrinsic value, a very real issue lies hidden. Depending on where the individual stands, attitudes differ to the question of the nature of history,

19

the importance of political life, the value of seeking ethical solutions to sociopolitical problems, the concern for national and
international justice, and the rights of the human being. In
other words, it may be that being religious or not ultimately has
to do with what we choose to believe about God; nevertheless,
it is in the world of human beings that the belief has to be im-
plemented. Our understanding of the world is the cash value
of our concept of God.

The unbeliever has a perfectly consistent position which
can be maintained without serious difficulty. If there is no God,
then human life and human achievements are not only the
expression of ultimate values; they are also the source of these
ultimate values. Human beings are both agents and judges of
value. Those things which human beings hold dear—life, freedom, material well-being, love, friendship—are held to be the
absolute values of existence. But if we proceed to ask *why* these
values are ultimate, the weakness of the unbeliever's position
soon emerges. If human beings are not the expression of something bigger than themselves, but the expression of something
of which they are the source, then there is a circularity in the
argument. The most important values in the world are those
values which human beings collectively hold to be of highest
importance. However, words such as "good" or "right" are
used of these values, or they may be said to "maximize happiness." The use of such terms as "good" or "right" means either
that an absolute has surreptitiously slipped into the discussion,
or that sheer human agreement has become the index of value.
Either religion or the tyranny of the majority.

Those who believe in a God but restrict the life of faith to
a vertical relationship of the individual to the divine which
has no essential connection with life in the world are placed
at the opposite extreme. Absolute value is given to the relationship with God, which is wholly a thing of God's creation,
and all else—which means the whole of everyday life—
has no intrinsic importance. The logical theoretical conclu-

20

sion of this, of course, is that anything goes, and there have certainly been those who held that freedom from the law meant that it did not matter in the last analysis *what* human beings did. However, it is more usual for the perils of possible lawlessness to force those who hold to the disjunction between God and human beings into an undignified scramble for a more than usually rigid moral dogmatism. In the scriptures, divine revelation speaks across the gulf with a series of precepts for the Christian life. These precepts tend to be taken literally, resulting in the establishment of a new legalism more stringent, though perhaps more selective, than the old. This group is obviously threatened by any undermining of the authority of Scripture.

An alternative and certainly more challenging view, adopted by a section of the Reformers' tradition, is that of an absolute but contentless claim of God upon the individual. God's claim or demand is for faith, not for assent to a series of propositions. The scriptural language in which this is clothed is a mythological interpretation, and therefore needs to be demythologized. This pattern is most closely associated with the advocacy of some form of Christian existentialism, and it deserves respect, but it falls under the general criticism of the group, that the autonomy of the world is finally a denial of the value of creation in general, and human existence in particular.

The incarnationalist is placed in the most complex position. On the one hand, history must be taken seriously. The world has changed, and will continue to change, and our ideas about everything, including God and God's relation to the world, are just as likely to be influenced by our historical situation as any other attitude we may have to anything else. The scriptures, therefore, are indeed the major source of Christian revelation, but they are also a series of historical documents, as subject to historical criticism and as potentially fallible in their historical judgments as any other. On the other hand, the incarnationalist is committed to what is apparently a totally

21

anachronistic attitude—a belief that a human being was God. The incarnationalist subscribes to the statement that Jesus Christ was a human being of whom it is equally true to say, "He is God." It is important to appreciate that the thorough-going commitment of the incarnationalist to the historically conditioned nature of all knowledge extends to this central and most cherished judgment. The belief in the incarnation may not be made a special case.

Before we go on to see how the incarnationalist position vis-à-vis Jesus Christ is defended, we should note that *if* the seemingly contradictory standpoint can be maintained, then its practical value is immense. It leads to a consistent and easily-defended attitude to the world. On the one hand, the values of the world and human life can be given their full weight as values in a world in which God has lived: that is, God, when human, subscribed to these values. On the other hand, they are values which God has found human beings esteeming in their world. They are human values, mandated by divine subjection to them, and as with values so with the subjects who conform to them. The intrinsic value of human beings is revealed by the fact that God in Jesus Christ was a human being, and God could not become something of no value without contradicting the divine nature. On the other hand, we are not God though we have beheld God in history. Human beings and their values are thus of intrinsic, if not absolute, worth.

Unbelievers and incarnationalists agree in setting a high value upon history; this, incidentally, is why Latin American Christians and Marxists can collaborate on many matters. The difference is that the unbeliever can say this only from inside history, and therefore the judgment is really an assertion. The incarnationalist is suggesting that the assertion of the value of history is supported by the emergence of an historical point of transcendent value *within* history. Jesus Christ is that point, and is therefore the validation of history. The unbeliever settles proudly, honorably, perhaps stoically, but certainly unsteadily, for a self-validation.

It is, of course, entirely possible to challenge the conclusions of the incarnationalist. After all, it might be argued, although the shape of the position is convincing, and although *if* Jesus Christ is divine, then his human existence was the validation of history, *that* he is divine is just as much an assertion as the atheistic claim that all value is a human projection. We need, consequently, to seek a deeper justification for the claims made for Jesus of Nazareth, before turning to the question of the political implications of these claims.

In the first place, it is necessary to stress that the incarnational views of Christianity begin from the human being. The central claim of Christianity is often stated in the form "God became man," but not sufficiently frequently in the equally true formulation, "a human being was God." The former is always beyond any kind of substantiation in history; we cannot start from God's point of view and see how God "descended" to the world. But it is in the world that Christian witness occurs, and the faith response grew out of the experience of God in the world. It was the man Jesus about whom they came to say, "he is Lord and God." This second formulation, then, asserts and emphasizes the presence of God in history in Jesus Christ. God is visible in Jesus Christ, not through a glass darkly, not reflected into the world through a lens, but as the significance of the history of this man. We can use the metaphor of translation; God is in history in Jesus Christ, translated into the language of humanity. The reality is the same: only the means of communication is different. It is a form of communication chosen, in fact dictated, by the nature of those with whom the communication is to be effected.

In focusing on Jesus Christ, we really have a choice between emphasizing the divinity of this man or the humanity of this God. In Christian tradition the divine man has received the larger share of attention; a concern more for the human God is today's attempt to redress the balance. And this emphasis is understandable if we reflect for a moment on the implications of the two approaches. "Divine man" suggests an ordinary human being who has somehow been invested with supernatural powers or divine status, a crossbreed of Superman and a Roman emperor. But neither of these pictures fits what we know of Jesus. For the most part he lived in obscurity, and then for a time as teacher and prophet. He had something of a following for a brief period, and he died a death of weakness and shame. At no time did he claim divinity for himself, if we are to accept the present critical consensus. And at no time during his life did his disciples claim divinity for him.

More importantly, it is obviously only true that a human being is God if the person about whom we say this really is a human being. Otherwise, we should in fact be saying that the being who seems to be a human being is in fact not a human being, but God. The humanity then becomes a disguise, and the human life a charade. That is not what Christians claim, though it may often seem to be implied by some of their beliefs. The claim, if not the reality, is beyond doubt: this man is God. Therefore we are in fact emphasizing the complete humanity as much as we are the divinity. Once again, this was stressed by the Fathers of the Council of Chalcedon. The impact of what we are saying is that the divine is mediated to history in the human—or, to put it a little more picturesquely, the shape that the divine takes in history is the human, the fully human, with all that that implies, as the human is revealed in its perfection in Jesus of Nazareth.

Focus on the human has traditionally raised such questions as that of the sinlessness of Jesus. How can a human being be sinless, or how can God be a sinner? Of course, the sinlessness of Jesus is founded precisely on the assertion of his *full* humanity. The full revelation of God in human terms requires full humanity, but full humanity is unimpeded hu-

24

manity, and since human sinfulness is at root the willful corruption or contradiction of human nature, so the perfect man, Jesus, must be sinless. Although this is logical enough, its strength has to arise from attention to the concrete life of Jesus of Nazareth. Further, the human God is possessed of all the limitations that pertain to human existence. The human God had to be born, could not just descend; had to learn, could not just know; had to be sinless through temptation, not lack of it; had to die, not evaporate. If God was to be in history, then the Revealer/Redeemer was going to be less than omniscient, less than all-powerful, less than immortal. Jesus' insight into human hearts was psychological insight, not divine prescience, and his vision extended no further than that of his disciples to the future existence of the jet engine or the possibilities of nuclear fission.

A rigorous emphasis on the humanity of the Redeemer leads to the assertion that there is no essential conflict between human and divine nature. Jesus Christ is the proof of that, and whatever it was in his humanity that made such a union possible is something all human beings share in principle, in virtue of sharing the same human nature. In principle, we can all reveal the divine, and most of us do so in shadowy ways from time to time. At the same time, in practice, we all fail to do so. Human nature in other words is potentially and implicitly at one with and therefore revelatory of the divine, but existentially hampered from its successful fulfillment. This restriction is in fact the limitation of the divine revelation by its subjection to the mediation of human agents. One of the questions we have to ask of a political theology is if it is true that "building the kingdom," or engaging in political praxis, is the way to overcome this "original sin."

The theoretical lengths we have gone to in this chapter have been necessary in order to make it clear what we are and are not talking about when we concern ourselves with incarnational theology. We are considering the implications of reflection on the concrete history of Jesus for human possibility now. But we can now put such issues to one side, and pose the question of the role of incarnation in building a political theology.

I take it as axiomatic that human life and history are of immense value. In consequence, the only theological positions I consider worth investigating are those which build a value for history into their outlook. As we saw above, this really leaves us with only two possible options: either history is entirely autonomous, with its own scale of values, and "comes of age" as radically independent of the divine, or it is the arena of the self-expression of the divine, and therefore the recognition of the oneness of human and religious values. Only the second of these two outlooks preserves the absoluteness of God and the dignity of the human. The former limits God to the beyond and relativizes secular values.

The incarnation is the doctrine which grounds the absoluteness of human history, and therefore that upon which any exaltation of political praxis must ultimately rest. Political praxis is either tinkering with the machinery of the state, or society's expression in its own concrete structures of what it takes to be finally important. The Christian vision which views world and God as radically divergent from one another sees the political as machinery for the preservation of rights and the encouragement of the fulfillment of duties. It is therefore essentially static and conservative. The view of the political as the concrete expression of the command to be "other Christs," and to incarnate the values of the kingdom, is of its nature dynamic because it involves a movement in a direction which never reaches its goal. And it can only have that status because of the "high anthropology" which a christology from below carries in its train.

Secondly, the incarnation balances the assertion of a divine human being and a human divinity, and, in the present-day necessity of countering the traditional overemphasis on the

26

former, incarnational theology stresses an entirely healthy recourse to experience. In this case, experience points to a starting-point in the concrete history of Jesus. It was Jesus' personal
history, and his reflection on it, which led to his own sense of
his mission. Subsequently, it was the reflection of others on
their own experience of Jesus which led to the confident assertion of his messiahship, and subsequently his divinity. The
whole process by which Jesus comes to be proclaimed as Lord
and God has its indispensable starting-point in the concrete
history of Jesus of Nazareth. That is ultimately the only justification for his proclamation as the Christ.

Of its nature the term "christology" directs us to the
Christian revelation, and it is the uniqueness of Christianity
that history is interpretative of the divine. The New Testament and subsequent reflection show a process in which Jesus
of Nazareth is the standard by which the term Christ is understood, and Jesus Christ is he through whom God's presence
among human beings is interpreted. This is a bold claim. Nevertheless, the alternative is to envisage the proclamation of Jesus
as Lord in terms of his fitting exactly into the preconceptions of
the Messiah held by the Jewish community. Whereas, of course,
the mystery and challenge of Jesus' Messianic ministry was that
it was not what was expected. Consequently, when Jesus was
proclaimed as the Christ for the first time, the symbol "Christ"
was modified. If this man with this particular history is the
Christ, as we believe (so the reasoning must have run), then we
must incorporate the following ideas into "Christ" and perhaps
put a question mark against some of the aspects we have long
thought to be central to the concept of Messiah.

Just as the history of a concrete individual is interpretative
of the Christ-symbol, so the resultant christology modifies the
notion of God. The process is identical at both stages. The community holds its beliefs about God. But if it is going on to say
that this Jesus who is the Christ is also God then it is going to
have to adjust its ideas about who God is. In particular, its God

must now become a reality which can be expressed and revealed in a human life. Through such stretchings of the minds and faiths of the believing community, God's revelation communicates itself in history.

The incarnation is thus a doctrine which is based entirely on a recourse to history, and to human experience. Political theology in its turn cannot exist comfortably with any other starting-point. In fact, one of the leading exponents of christology from a liberation-theology perspective, Jon Sobrino, explicitly defends the emphasis on the concrete history of Jesus as an escape from the distortions of theoretical or abstract christology. This general methodological option of reality over ideology, as we shall see throughout this book, is fundamental to political and liberation theology, and axiomatic in a true christology. It is of course also highly problematic, since any recourse to this historical Jesus is severely limited by the problems of uncovering that history. Two points are therefore important: the first is that it is necessary to assert the historicity of the starting-point of the subsequent reflection and belief which we find recorded in the New Testament; and the second is to practice a radical ideology critique of the texts to try to uncover the events which lie behind the interpretative overlay. This does not have to be naïve.

Finally and most importantly, incarnational theology is simultaneously parent and child of an anthropology which can support a theology of hope, which grounds a belief in the limitlessness of human possibility, and which can talk in the same breath about building the kingdom and building the human community. We said a little way back that a christology from below ends with a high anthropology. If a human being is truly God, then human nature is no mean thing. In principle, it can be unified with the divine, or, more functionally expressed, it can be the representation of the divine in history. This "can be" is not mindless optimism, head-burying in theological sand to avoid the painful realities of a world in which human beings

28

certainly do not behave as if they have any likeness to the divine. Rather, it is the sober recognition that what has been can be again. Incarnational theology issues in an ecclesiology in which human beings, with all their possibilities, seek to be "other Christs" to their own particular world. In being true to their human nature, which means of course true to the human community, they *are* the presence of Christ in the world. The ecclesiology of the true incarnational theology, a community struggling for authentic humanity despite the internal and external pressures to compromise, is one whose endeavor must of its nature find its home in political activity within the human community. Materialism and fearfulness muddy the springs of political action and blur the image of Christ.

3

God's Fidelity and Human Commitment

MANY DIFFERENT CHRISTIAN CHURCHES include a profession of faith in their religious services. These "creeds" can easily be broken down into a set of individual propositions—"articles of faith," as they are often known. For such phrases wars have been fought, throats have been slit, and heretics have been burned at the stake. Although we no longer kill one another for religious motives, the creeds remain for very many people the central articulation of the Christian faith.

The way in which the creeds were formulated can mislead us as to their purpose. They are not the rule of membership for the Christian club. In fact, "they" are not one thing at all; the character of the individual propositions varies so much. That is to say, they are not all intended in the same way: "I believe in Jesus Christ who . . . suffered under Pontius Pilate" is a plain historical claim about the individual at the origin of Christianity. "I believe in the holy, catholic, and apostolic Church" is a reference to a visible institution which even on the very highest ecclesiology does not rank with Jesus Christ as object of faith. Other statements are presentations of truth through symbolic or metaphorical forms of expression: thus, "maker of heaven and earth," and the "Holy Spirit . . . the giver of life." Still others are the incorporation of subtle theological issues into the profession: "God from God, light from light, true God from true God, begotten not made, of one being with the Father," or that most highly controversial claim that the Holy Spirit proceeds "from the Father *and* the Son."

There is not only a problem about the various kinds of affirmations in the creeds, there is also the peculiarly modern unease with "creeds" at all. What happens when we recite the creed? Are we in fact simply hearing a lot of sentences strung together by the Church, which demands our agreement to the resulting document? And if we mumble the bits we do not like or take a deep breath while they are being said so that we do not actually have to pronounce the offending words, are we cheating? At the opposite end of the scale, there is the assumption that no set of ancient words and formulae can possibly have any relation to modern life in today's world, and the consequent decision to discard them and start afresh with modern insights. Both these views make the same fundamental mistake; neither understands the kind of thing that a creed *is*.

A creed is not a set of rules for membership. God will not strike us down for temporary unease about some aspect of the communion of saints, or even for not being entirely sure what it means to say that Jesus Christ is "light from light." Nor, on the other hand, is it a set of insights, and can therefore not be replaced by modern insights without destroying something irreplaceable.

As a profession of faith, the creed has two aspects: it is a recital of God's faithfulness toward the human race, and it is an affirmation of God's major act in history. To explain this, we need to turn to a close examination of biblical faith.

OLD TESTAMENT FAITH

The greater part of the book of Deuteronomy takes the form of a long sermon by Moses, explaining the law of God to the Israelites. Chapter 26 includes a summary of the faith of Israel:

> A wandering Aramean was my father, and he went down into Egypt and sojourned there, few in number; and there he became a nation, great, mighty and populous. And the Egyptians treated us harshly, and afflicted us, and laid upon us hard bondage. Then we cried to the Lord the God of our Fathers, and the Lord heard our

voice, and saw our affliction, our toil, and our oppressions; and the Lord brought us out of Egypt with a mighty hand and an outstretched arm, with great terror, with signs and wonders; and he brought us into this place and gave us this land, a land flowing with milk and honey [Deut. 26:5–9].

This creed, like the Old Testament as a whole, makes no mention of the nature of God. It is concerned only with the deeds of God, and, although the point can be exaggerated, it is fair to describe this as the distinctively Hebrew attitude to God. Its thrust is similar to the old tag that philosophers sometimes use—"Don't ask for the meaning, ask for the use!" In other words, God is to be known only where God is visible, and this is in history, where God intervenes on behalf of the chosen people.

Old Testament faith is, then, in the first place a trust in the God of "our Fathers." God is always identified as "the God of Abraham, of Isaac, and of Jacob," and it is this historical formula rather than any speculative or philosophical definition that identifies Yahweh. It also has the advantage of referring back to those patriarchal figures who represent supreme types of trust in God. Abraham, for example, spent his life in constant upheaval, on the move throughout Egypt and Canaan, at the behest of God, who from time to time in the Genesis account renews the promise to make of him "the father of many nations." Abraham's trust in God finally succumbs to skeptical laughter when God seems to promise the impossible: "Then Abraham fell on his face and laughed and said to himself: 'Shall a child be born to a man who is a hundred years old? Shall Sarah, who is ninety years old, bear a child?' " But all happens as God has promised, and Sarah gives birth to Isaac, with whom God is to continue his covenant. God has been faithful because Abraham has trusted in God. The further story of Abraham's trust in God when he has been ordered to sacrifice Isaac is too well-known to need repetition here. The point of the story (which can seem negative and destructive to the modern

33

mind) is that perfect trust in God is repaid by God's perfect fidelity to the promise.

The God of Abraham, of Isaac, and of Jacob is a God who makes demands in the context of a promise. To trust that God is to have faith in God, and the faith is vindicated in God's faithfulness to the promises. The promise in itself is a promise to *do* something for the faithful, to act on their behalf, to intervene in their history, or to protect them. This is the measure of Old Testament faith: to trust in the faithfulness of Yahweh, evidenced in Yahweh's dealings with the faithful in the past, and expressed in the continuing promise of the covenant. This is why the quotation from Deuteronomy is important; it expressed the faith of Israel about the bond that God was taken to have struck with Israel through Moses, long before the time at which Deuteronomy was written. The covenant was a kind of treaty between God and the people of Israel; trust in and obedience to God would be met by God's loving protection. The core narrative of the Old Testament takes this covenant to be the center of the history of the chosen people. Their history revolves around their periodic unfaithfulness. When this occurs, God punishes them by withdrawing protection for a time, and they are overrun by one of their neighbors, or taken into captivity, or left at the mercy of hostile armies. When they return or are brought back to faithfulness, often as a result of harsh treatment from their enemies, they find their God there to welcome them back into the covenant bond.

The great prophetic movement of Judaism is a tradition of individuals, called by God to recall the people to their covenantal responsibilities. The prophets appear at times when Israel has fallen away, and their harsh message is always the unwelcome reminder of the tradition that has been forgotten. But just as persistent as the harshness of their judgment is the sense of God's "steadfast" or "abiding" love, God's faithfulness to the house of Israel. If we reverse the usual practice, and take a New Testament story to shed light on Old Testament theology, the pattern of the covenantal relationship is very much like that between father and younger son in the parable of the Prodigal Son. God, like the father in the story, has always loved and protected, yet leaves the child free to rebel. And when the child returns in true penitence, God is there to welcome the sinner back as though that sin had never been, time and time again. That is the message of the covenantal theology of the Old Testament: it teaches the lesson of *trust in God's faithfulness to Israel.*

There is a second and equally important dimension to Old Testament faith. The believer's relationship with God is not simply a trust in God's promise and God's fidelity to that promise, but a trust that the fidelity will involve God's acting in history to fulfill the promise. The God of the Old Testament is a God who is primarily visible and known in the events of history, a God who can even act in history through unwitting agents— the pagan king Cyrus of Persia, for example, was an agent of the divine purpose in the release of Israel from the Babylonian exile.

It is possible to overstate the distinction between Greek and Hebrew ways of thinking in the background to the Christian tradition, and it is even more tempting to dismiss the one in favor of the other, usually the Greek, for being "too abstract." Nevertheless it is true to say that the Greek dimension of the Christian tradition would give more emphasis to seeking to *understand* God, and hence to coming close in some way to an appreciation of the *nature* of God. It is to the Greek tradition that we owe our theology of the Trinity, with its distinction between persons and natures. For Hebrew ways of thinking, the nature of God is unknowable and mysterious: "theophanies" or divine appearances in the Old Testament are invariably shrouded in mystery. You cannot discover much about the nature of God from investigating a burning bush, for example; and the angels of the Old Testament tradition, by the fact that they stand as messengers between divine and human, are indicators of and contributors to the mysterious character of Yahweh. In this tradition, understanding is found not in philosophical investigation of the nature of God but in looking upon and praising the works of God in the world. It is not the nature of God that is knowable, but the *effects* of God. Through the divine plan, the divine personality is revealed.

God's record in history is the principal evidence for God's fidelity to the covenant. God protects and blesses the chosen people, insofar as they too pursue faithfulness to the covenant. Consequently, and most importantly, Israel is not interested primarily in a God who will reward the faithful for a life of obedience to divine commands by showering eternal happiness on him or her in the "next" life, but a God who is loving and generous here and now through acting in history to protect and care for the faithful. Such a viewpoint is particularly vulnerable, of course, for there is inevitably so much evidence in history of the apparent neglect of the chosen people by their God. This problem of suffering is examined at length in the Old Testament, especially in the Book of Job and in the Psalms, and it is a matter which has persisted throughout the history of the Jewish people, almost as if God were mocking their belief in God's willingness to act on their behalf. The Holocaust has been their severest challenge to date. Throughout their history, however, they seem to have preferred an almost perversely blind trust in God's act in history to the recourse of some otherworldly reward for the pains of the here and now.

THE FAITH OF JESUS

Once upon a time, it would have seemed a shocking idea to suggest that Jesus had to have any faith at all. After all, if he was God surely he *knew* and so did not need to *believe*? However, we have already made reference in the last chapter to the crucial point that if we take the Christian tradition seriously

Jesus Christ's full humanity has to be emphasized, that being human in Jesus Christ was God's way of being divine in history. Consequently, as a full human being the problem of faith must have presented itself to him in terms parallel to those of his contemporaries. The history of how to overcome that problem, through the trials and sacrifices to which his faith led him, is the history of God in history.

If the status of the faith of Jesus is so exalted, what was the character of that faith? It was a human faith in God, and the faith of a particular historical person, and so it should be describable and appreciable, even though at this distance in time from the life of Jesus of Nazareth it may not be easy to go into detail with any guarantee of accuracy. The fact that we have to attempt to obtain some idea of it bears witness to the importance of the role of the "historical Jesus" in the thinking of political theology. Jesus' way of being in the world was his political role, just as much as if he had lived in the twentieth century and run for Senate or House. The hope and expectation in inquiring into Jesus' faith is that it was closely allied to his attitude to the society in which he lived.

Investigating the faith of Jesus is a matter of looking into his life, as far as we can uncover it after two thousand years. We must avoid becoming abstract; we could decide, for example, that Jesus' faith was exactly the Old Testament trust in God's actions, and look no further. We could designate him "the perfectly obedient one." We might settle for describing him as the "incarnate Word." All these formulations, and many others, have something to recommend them, but they all suffer from being abstractions. They must not be allowed to take priority over the fact that as an historical person Jesus had a concrete history. A personal history, for every human being, means change, conflict, and development. It means growth in experience and wisdom and understanding. Consequently, we cannot isolate Jesus' faith as if it were a quality or essence that he possessed *ab ovo*. Instead, and this direction is stressed by Jon Sobrino in *Christology at the Crossroads*,[1] we are trying to uncover *the history of the faith of Jesus*.

Given what we have come to believe about Jesus, we obviously want to say that his faith was perfect. But what does it mean to say that someone has perfect faith? It does not mean that there is a steady certitude. The possession of faith (which is not objective or scientific knowledge) implies a need for faith, and faith is possessed hazardously in the face of successive life-crises. Faith, even that of Jesus, is always a struggle with doubt. A perfect faith, then, is a fidelity to God's covenant, and a trust in God's activity in history on our behalf, held in the teeth of sinfulness and suffering, and maintained despite the temptation to reject it which these existential problems inevitably bring. And of course if faith is fidelity, then it is of its nature historical; it is part of a process, and its character can be assessed truly only at the end of the struggle, only at the moment of triumph. The triumph of fidelity is the death of the believer; all that precedes that, however spectacular or however apparently perfect, can be only provisional.

The characteristics of the history of the faith of Jesus are not easily discernible in the gospels. The term "faith" is rarely used of Jesus himself, although the remark in the Letter to the Hebrews that Jesus is "the pioneer and perfecter of our faith" (Heb. 12:2) is very helpful. Overall, the paucity of references discourages too exact a schema for Jesus' growth in faith, but there are hints enough to offer a few suggestions. In the first place, for example, we can be relatively confident that Jesus inherited his understanding of faith from the prophetic Jewish tradition in which he so clearly stood. He would have seen faith as a trust in the fidelity of God to the covenant bond, understanding this as a promise to act on behalf of a faithful Israel. He would have believed that trust in God should show itself in obedience to the commands of God. More personally, Jesus must have seen his own mission in terms of his fidelity to what

God seemed to be asking of him, once again on the prophetic pattern. He may have been reluctant to follow what he must have seen would be a difficult path in life, but, once convinced that it was God's will, he would have had no real alternative.

Jesus' inherited understanding of faith as fidelity and trust must be set against a personal history of hardship, suffering, rejection, and apparent failure. This too is characteristic of the prophet. In other words, the history of his faith is not one of serene assurance, but of the maintenance of fidelity and trust in the face of severe existential crisis. The New Testament picture of that severity varies from Gospel to Gospel; Mark's Gospel probably presents it at its starkest, John's at its most muted. But whichever way we read it, he was undoubtedly much misunderstood, deserted by his closest followers, at least for a time, subjected to beatings and an unfair trial, and executed in a hideous and humiliating fashion, as if he were a common criminal. Like the writers of Psalms 38 and 39, Jesus was a righteous man apparently deserted by God, and like those writers his response was to continue to trust that God would act. The resurrection and the subsequent impact of Jesus Christ are, if nothing else, God's vindication of Jesus.

Jesus did not have to wait for death to see God acting in the world in pursuance of the divine part of the covenantal bargain. Although Jesus may not have appreciated it at the time, his personal history was itself the triumphant act of God in the world, the revelation of God's self in human history. In other words, faith in the face of conflict is the divine way of being in the world. But besides this, Jesus had evidence enough of God's acting in the world through his own words and deeds. This point is vitally important. Many fine words and many miracles are recorded of Jesus, and, although we cannot be sure of the literal authenticity of many of them, we can affirm that some teaching and some healing lie behind the unprecedented personal impact of this man, and be equally certain that he did not lay it to his own account but accepted, once again in prophetic mold, that this was the work of God through him. We also know that his charge to his followers to go and preach the word demonstrated the assurance that others could work great deeds in the name of God. The acts of God in the world in Jesus' time, in other words, were the acts of Jesus and his disciples, and were also the acts of the Jewish and Roman authorities who at moments, like Cyrus before them, were unwitting instruments of God's self-revelation in history.

Jesus' faithfulness to God is coterminous with his faithfulness to the kingdom or reign of God. He knew that proclaiming the kingdom was his God-given role, and that he was bound to fidelity to that mission. He also believed that God acted in history. Consequently, although there is no need or justification for asserting Jesus' awareness of the supreme significance of his own life, there is every reason to assume that he saw that life as one history through which God was acting in the world. And if as we must suppose Jesus reflected deeply on the nature of his mission, his understanding of the character of the reign of God and of the role of his own weakness and failure in its successful proclamation must have developed during the years of his ministry. In fact, faithfulness despite apparent failure is far more a revelation of the way of God in history than are miracles and triumphs.

THE FAITH OF THE CHRISTIAN

The faith of the New Testament is a trust in the revelation of God through the life of Jesus Christ: the faith of the contemporary Christian is essentially the same. Therefore, as we take up the biblical fidelity into our own faith, we have to begin by asserting that faith is trust in God's promises to act on our behalf. To that distinctively biblical and prophetic picture we have now to add the characteristic Christian insight. Christian faith involves trust in God's supreme fulfillment of the promise in the life and death of Jesus Christ. Jesus, the Son of God, is God's way of making open to us in human history our way to God. The history of Jesus' own faith is the pattern of the Christian life—trust in God and God's acts in history, in the face of existential difficulties.

Our biblical faith as Christians is not a mere repetition of the faith of the Old Testament, but strengthens, clarifies, and transforms it. Because of the status we discern in faith in Jesus, because we talk of him as the incarnate one, which is a way of saying that he was the full presentation by God of the way to come to God in history, so we can be persuaded anew of the dignity and importance of all human beings. Since we humans share our human nature with the fully human Jesus, so the chosen medium of God's self-revelation to us is as close to us as our own humanity. And so, finally, we come to see that the means of God's activity in history is the power of human agency. Jesus' perfect cooperation with God resulted in the perfect presence of God in history. God was manifest in Jesus; the history of the life of Jesus is the history of God's presence in the world in a single historical individual. God's continued presence and actions in history is in the power of the Spirit, which *is* in the world nowhere but in the life and faith of human beings.

Let us go back over this crucial but difficult point one more time. In the Old Testament we saw many figures expressing their trust in God's actions in history, and we have a great deal of evidence that God acted through individuals, whether through the historical role of the enemies of Israel or through the direct intervention of the prophets and patriarchs. These were ordinary human beings who became for a time agents of God. They did great things in pursuance of God's relationship with the chosen people. These instances of God's activity in the Old Testament fitted into no general theory or explanation of the relationship of God to the agents of the divine will. This became available only when reflection on the perfect divine agent followed the death and resurrection of Jesus Christ. His

41

perfect agency, his perfect representation of God, was the presence of God in history. But it was a human presence too, and thus it became apparent that all those who have a human nature are at least able in principle to be involved in the work of God in the world. Jesus showed that God was not distant from and totally other than creation. So, the agency of the patriarchs, prophets, and enemies of Israel in the Old Testament was not a matter of isolated individuals chosen rather capriciously to carry out some divine plan, but simply the visible tip of the iceberg. The enemies of Israel and pagan allies like Cyrus show that human history can be the vehicle of God's loving care. And the patriarchs and prophets demonstrate that human beings who are trusting in and faithful to God are themselves doing the work of God. This is the truth available when we reflect on the history of Israel and the history of Jesus. Trust and fidelity, on the one hand, and doing the work of God, on the other, are the marks of the true believer. The one will not exist without the other.

This relationship between trust in God and doing the work of God is supremely evident in Jesus' life. There, it takes the form of what we have called his faithfulness to God and to God's kingdom. Jesus proclaimed the coming of the kingdom through progressively more difficult trials, out of trust in God's protection, confident that he was doing God's work even when he failed. John's Gospel brings out best the sense of the oneness of the actions of Jesus and God: "He who believes in me believes not in me but in him who sent me. And he who sees me sees him who sent me" (Jn. 14).

To conclude this section, let us try to sketch out what the faith of the contemporary Christian looks and feels like. It is a faith which has two major points of reference—the everyday world and the scriptures—and it is a faith set against one background, that of the community in which the Christian lives. To consider the background of the community first, the same theological reflection on the incarnation which leads the Christian to see his or her actions done in faith as God's actions in the world, leads to a like reverence for the actions of others. Thinking about our world reveals the importance of the social, cultural, and economic network for giving us birth, nurturing our attitudes, educating us, and sometimes impeding our honest attempts to face the world. Our community, in the form of people or the attitudes we share with them, is always with us. Consequently, if we look at our faith as a private affair between ourselves and God, we are misunderstanding it. The mistake is not a mistake about God, for no doubt God speaks to us as individuals, and acts through us as individuals. But it is a mistake in understanding the world, for we are there and act there first and last as members of a community.

The two points of reference of our faith—the world and the scriptures—will come in for closer scrutiny in chapter five of this book. For the moment, we need to note only that the Christian believer will look to the Bible for the *history* of faith— that of Israel and that of Jesus himself—and find it there as a struggle to remain faithful to God and a trust in God's activity in the world. The divine activity is seen in the Bible as human activity. This biblical picture stands in close relationship, although one which needs and will receive a fuller elaboration, to the canvas of our contemporary world. There must be both consonance and challenge between the two.

ORTHOPRAXIS

I have saved this strange and probably unfamiliar word until now, for fear of frightening some of my readers away. The word is important in political theology, but it is in fact a peculiar word to describe a fairly familiar idea, or at least an idea which I hope will not seem too strange coming at the end of this particular chapter. "Orthopraxis" in fact means "right action." It is a word used to describe a certain attitude to faith, and it is best clarified by comparison with the word "orthodoxy."

To consider orthodoxy we need to go back to where we began this chapter, with traditional understandings of faith. Faith, we said, consisted in agreeing to the articles of the creed, abiding by the rules of the particular organization—in this case, the Church. If you kept the rule, you were orthodox: if not, you were heterodox or heretical. Orthodoxy was the test of faith, but orthodoxy meant right doctrine or right opinion. In other words, faith was tested by a profession, by something said, and in itself had no connection with action. It is clearly an idea which is far removed from the biblical idea of faith as we have outlined it.

A very familiar New Testament saying is the one that insists that those who enter the kingdom of heaven will be not the ones who protest their faith in cries of "Lord, Lord!" but those who keep quiet and get on with *doing* the will of God. This illustrates the basic difficulty with a univocal appeal to orthodoxy as a test of faith. Of course, it is likely to be true that the really good, struggling Christian will be found within the ranks of those who hold their tradition in high honor, and have come to their contemporary faith in dialogue with what they have inherited, but this is not to say that a slavish repetition of the words of the creed guarantees that one is living a Christian life. The point is one of simple logic: to say that all good Christians are orthodox is not to say all orthodox are good Christians. Therefore, it is not satisfactory to base an assessment of faith, particularly one's own, on one's personal claim to believe. Words are not enough.

It is also true that a deep personal conviction of a religious experience of conversion or of discovering Jesus as one's "personal Saviour" is not sufficient in itself for the possession of a saving faith. It may of course be a personally valuable experience, but real validity will result in a conversion in one's attitude to society.

Political theology does not ask Christianity to discard the role of right belief. It simply asks that *right action* rather than *right belief* be made the test of Christian faith. Hence, some Latin American theologians talk about a "pre-reflective commitment to the oppressed." This phrase, about which we shall hear more later, suggests that the good action is a truer test of faith than the mere verbal claim to believe. Our investigations of biblical faith would tend to support that conclusion.

However, the call for right action is not sufficient in itself as a test of faith. There are a number of reasons for this. Firstly, of course, right action is entirely possible for someone who holds none of the truths of Christianity. You do not have to be a Christian to see that in some countries the oppression of the people is such that all men and women with any courage and morality must unite with the oppressed to struggle for justice. The Christian may see this as an integral part of the endeavor to bring about the kingdom of God, but it will not necessarily change the quality of the Christian's actions. In fact, many non-Christians, whether atheists or members of some other religion, are capable of much more sustained right action than many Christians.

The more important problem, however, has to do with the discernment of right action. It may indeed be obvious in some societies that identification with the oppressed is a major priority for Christians. It may be equally true in all societies. But there is no doubt that identifying the oppressed in any particular society may be much more problematic. And having successfully identified the group or groups of society, the question arises: what does my need to identify with the oppressed *in fact* demand of me? What form must this alignment of my priorities take? Several competing and defensible strategies for the oppressed might be available, and they would all in a sense be "right action." The question of choosing between possible courses of action or the question of the direction of our right action reveals the insufficiency of considering orthopraxis to mean simply right action. Belief without action is empty: but action without belief is thrashing around in the dark.

Orthopraxis is better understood as the test of faith through the right relationship of belief and action. The two elements of trust in the promise of God and trust that God acts in history through the acts of human beings are held together on the biblical pattern. Praxis is not simply "practice" but the agreement of theory and practice. Of course such a relationship is reciprocal or circular and not a matter of one preceding the other. This circularity will be a matter of later discussion. For the moment let us take a brief look at the need for the ruling idea of orthopraxis in today's Church.

The fundamental criticism of the emphasis on orthodoxy is that over the centuries it has not protected the identity of belief and action, which is of course vital to the credibility of the Church to outsiders, and to its own self-respect. To make a perhaps over-simple comparison: it was the early Church in which Christians sought to express the principle of sharing which evoked the remark, "See how those Christians love one another!" It was the practical expression of love which showed through, just as, in human experience in general, real love is shown far better in the acceptance, generosity, and sacrifice which make up the lives of billions of human beings than in the more emotionally-charged moments which mark the early stages of such relationships. The Church of today, however, to its everlasting shame, demonstrates precisely the same divisions between people within its ranks as exist in the world as a whole. Some of the richest people in the world piously kneel in the churches of London, New York, Washington, Rio de Janeiro, Rome, and so on, while their brothers and sisters in Christ starve as they kneel and pray before the same God. The same God? Some Christians have nothing to eat, while others gorge themselves on what they do not need, and take health cures to cope with the effects of excess which themselves cost in a week far more than many of the world's poor can earn in an entire year. Consequently, can we blame people for the rejection of the Church, whether outsiders or some of those who were brought up in it? Are they guilty of short-sightedness, idealism, or just common sense? It seems clear that the short-sightedness lies with those of us (and that means most of us) who are perfectly content to see the socio-economic status quo of the world community mirrored in the lives of Christians.

Orthodoxy as the touchstone of faith is, then, largely discredited by its record. It may have preserved the faith in its purity, but it has kept very few of us pure in the faith. This is not because there is anything intrinsically wrong with the concept of "right belief" but because the demand for action that is as loud as the demand for belief has been underplayed by the churches as a whole. The churches, like individual Christians, select from and hence censor the gospel.

It is quite certain that the orthodoxy which results in this emasculated Christianity is a false orthodoxy, because a true orthodoxy would surely incorporate the inversion of the values of the status quo expressed in the Sermon on the Mount. More significantly still, a genuine orthodoxy would produce believers who followed the way to God shown in the history of Jesus' faith, and the history of his faith is composed of actions done in obedience in the face of great peril and conflict.

The traditional understanding of orthodoxy has not helped to produce a world which demonstrates with any clarity that Christians accept what is practical in Jesus' *incontrovertible* option for the poor, underprivileged, sick, crippled, blind, socially unfortunate, despised, and in general anyone whom society had pushed to the margins of its consciousness. In fact, it would be possible to make a good case for orthodoxy, as it has ruled our past, being a perhaps unwitting accomplice in the ease with which we Christians ignore such groups. But this situation is not simply a matter of human weakness; it also involves an important theological point.

One way of looking at the role of Christians in the world, which we have more than once hinted is connected with being agents of God at work in the world, is as the sacrament of the presence of Christ. By living the Christian life in all its dimensions, they *are* the visible presence of God in the world, they *are* the Holy Spirit, they *are* a re-presentation of Jesus Christ. Once again, this is not an ahistorical truth asserted as a doctrine of faith. It is *made true* by the history of the community and the individuals within it. It involves re-presenting not Jesus' *being*, as a kind of empty essence, but his *way of being*, his concrete life with all its priorities. At the same time, it does not involve adopting the ways or opinions of a first-century Jew. It is a representation in a different historical epoch of the orientation of Jesus' life.

The contemporary Christian cannot stop with the easy assent of orthodoxy, but must balance it with the harsh realities of orthopraxis. The Christian must seek a fundamental consonance between beliefs and way of being in the world today, and Jesus' way of being in his world. Because we have argued that orthopraxis is established when right action indicates the quality of faith and doctrine, so we must go on to assert the priority of action over belief. Action in alignment with the Christian commitment to building the kingdom, even if the action is that of an atheistic Marxist, contributes to that kingdom. But the empty proclamation of the kingdom without praxis directed toward its achievement is counter-productive, literally a scandal, a stumbling block to those who would share in the work.

NOTE

1. (Maryknoll: Orbis, 1978).

4

The Christian and History

WE FINISHED THE LAST CHAPTER in a discussion of ortho-praxis, and we commented there that the Christian life in to-day's world is not about trying to represent Jesus' essence or being but his way of being. This is perhaps fortunate, since the historical pattern of his life ought to be more accessible. How-ever, if we really want to represent Jesus Christ as he was in historical existence, we have to do so through the information we have about him from reliable witnesses. Once again, we face a familiar question in contemporary theology: how and what can we know about the facts of the historical existence of Jesus?

Theologians frequently distinguish the Jesus of history from the Christ of faith. The tradition, even the earliest scrip-tural accounts, in fact present reflections on the significance of the historical Jesus, and are in consequence already concerned with the Christ of faith. It is the Christ of faith who is met in the resurrection appearances of the Lord, and, in the early sermons of the apostles, the Jesus of history is presented as the Christ of faith. Political theology does not dismiss the Christ of faith, but feels the need to try to go behind to the historical Jesus to escape the traps into which the Christ of faith may lead—in particu-lar, the abstraction and ideologization that necessarily is in-corporated in the process of interpretation. This is not an easy task.

From one point of view, it is next to impossible to come to grips at all with the historical Jesus. Very little evidence of his existence is available from outsde the tradition and scriptures of the Christian Church. True, within the literature we have a mass of sayings and accounts of his doings, but contemporary Christian scholars are notoriously unwilling to pronounce on which or how many sayings can with certainty be attributed to Jesus himself, and find quite a number of the reported events of Jesus' life not to have taken place exactly as recorded. Hard, historical reportage is seemingly scarce.

If we look at the same evidence and opinion from a slightly different angle, we may arrive at a more hopeful picture. There is no outside witness to the historical existence of Jesus, but the phenomenon of Christianity itself is the best evidence of the incontrovertibility of that life. Against the odds, Christianity grew up in such a dramatic fashion and persisted despite the many pressures working against it that it cannot be successfully explained as either hoax or fraud. Again, the words and deeds of Jesus himself may have receded behind a veil of interpretation, but this is evidence of the community's concern to interpret the significance of the words of the one who gave meaning to its existence. The ornamentation of the deeds, the elaboration and ascription of sayings testify only to the profound importance of this man.

The lack of historical reliability of the sayings ascribed to Jesus and the exact details of many events recorded of his life in the Gospels raises a serious problem for orthopraxis. If orthopraxis has as its theological justification the drive to re-present Jesus' way of being in the world, how is that way of being to be uncovered? Of course, in some ways it is extremely useful that the words and deeds of Jesus are not known with more certainty; the less we know of brute fact, the less we are inclined to a wooden transfer of one century's way of thinking to another. What we have in the scriptures are early interpretations of what Jesus said and did, mixed, quite certainly, with some *ipsissima verba*, and with accounts of those central events (death, resurrection) which may be heavily overlaid with interpretation, but which must have occurred in some form for the man Jesus to

50

become significant in quite the way he did. The fact that we are dealing from the start with interpretation frees us from the tyranny of literalism.

There is a very sound tradition in the rules of interpretation that if you are faced with two possible readings of a text it is wiser to accept the one which is on the surface the less likely or "harder" reading. The thinking is that the less plausible reading would not be there unless it were authentic, while the more credible reading may well be an attempt to clear up the obscurities of the more difficult. Similarly, when we look at the Gospels as reflections on the significance of the life of Jesus during his active life of teaching and preaching, we are on the whole on firmer ground if we conclude that the evangelists are unlikely to have invented those parts of their accounts in which Jesus' behavior is strange, eccentric, subversive of established custom, or not accurately representative of the expected conduct of a religious leader. The miracles and the great sermons may well be accurate accounts, but the paradoxes, the parables, and the evident preference for the poor are more surely so.

What can we say with any confidence about Jesus' concrete options in his life? Clearly, he saw the fulfillment of his mission as more important than his comfort, safety, or popularity. He interpreted this mission as having been given to him by God, with whom he undoubtedly saw himself as having a particularly close relationship, although one in which there was certainly a demand for obedience as well as the gift of love. The mission was to proclaim although not necessarily to bring about the kingdom of God. The reign of God was to be characterized by an inversion of many established values of the world of the times: the belief that the law was absolute; the conviction that riches and security were the lot of those who followed the law and were hence favored by God; conversely, that those who were physically or socially handicapped in any way were being punished by God and were important to the favored only as recipients of those alms which the law enjoined them to give. As Jesus' public ministry progressed, it probably became increasingly clear to him that his identification with those who had no success in the world would be perfected to the point at which he would himself apparently fail. As this realization grew in one well-versed in the Jewish scriptures, it is quite possible that his struggle to understand may have led him, say, to a new appreciation of the suffering servant songs of Isaiah. With such an association could have come the beginnings of a realization of the exalted role that his obedient suffering had in God's work.

To present a portrait of Jesus as the suffering servant, who is inevitably condemned to death by a society whose values God has called him to challenge, is in some measure conjectural, especially when we suggest that he may have seen his own career in such terms. Nevertheless, it is plausible, orthodox, and defensible. The major difficulty arises from the fact that it is not the picture which the churches as a whole have presented of their "founder." This, by and large, is because they have taken the ontological to the exclusion of the existential path. They have been so concerned with the abstract being of Jesus Christ that they have omitted to give sufficient attention to the concrete history which, when all is said and done, is the evidence upon which the early community professed his divinity. The institutional churches have been so taken up with the divine nature and an almost magical view of its influence on history that Jesus' human history has faded in theological significance.

If my picture of Jesus' concrete choices is substantially accurate, or at least largely defensible, this does not mean that the problems of representing Jesus' orientation therewith evaporate. The emphasis in representation is on *re*-presentation. But it begins to make the re-presentation of Jesus at least approachable, since what we are about to attempt is the re-presentation of his way of being in the world, not of his nature. All the same, it does little more as it stands than bring us face to face with what has come to be called the hermeneutical problem. That is, in seeking to come to grips with Jesus of Nazareth as a historical personage, we may move in one of two directions. It is possible on the one hand that we will conclude that his historical existence has disappeared totally behind a wall of interpretation. If that is our conclusion we shall have nothing more to work with in trying to live the gospel now than a history of interpretation and our own attitudes, inherited or invented, to what that means in today's world. On the other hand, we may decide that some or all of the deeds and words of Jesus are available through the scriptures. But then, by definition, what we have are the words and deeds of someone who lived two thousand years ago, and the whole problem of the relationship between his way of being in the world and ours begins to come into focus. How can we know with any assurance what his world felt like to him, or what the motivation was behind his lived choices? And how do we make the transition from those choices then to our choices now? The problem is one of understanding or interpretation: it is a *hermeneutical* problem.

If we look closely at the history of interpretations which we commonly refer to as the teaching of the Church, we can see that a similar problem exists on a smaller scale. Between the events of Jesus' life and the first interpretation we have in our possession in the scriptural accounts, and between the scriptural accounts and subsequent interpretation, there is discontinuity. The gap in time may be large or small, but is often many centuries and rarely less than a few decades, and is usually compounded by vast cultural distances. With every new reader, in some way, the hermeneutical problem recurs. How can we be sure of the accurate transfer of ideas and facts across the ages and over the oceans? When I speak to you, or when you read what I have written here, the opportunities for misunderstanding are many, despite the fact that we probably share most cultural assumptions and much the same slot in history. How much more difficult it is for Augustine to read Paul, or Thomas

Aquinas or Luther to read Augustine, or Karl Barth or Hans
Küng to read Luther. The bigger the gap in time, the greater the
problem, but any gap in time brings in principle the same set of
difficulties.

HISTORY AND INTERPRETATION

It may seem as if I have presented the picture in such a gloomy
fashion that there is no point in going on, because no one can
know anything with any certainty. But there is no need to despair just yet, as the issue is based partially on a fallacy. The
problem is simply an illustration of the nature of history, "a
pattern of timeless moments," as T. S. Eliot called it. If we ask
ourselves the question whether history is a lot of moments, each
separate from the other, or a fluid continuum, it takes only a
little reflection to see that in different ways it is both. If there
is any reality to the word "now" there must be moments, but if
I can remember what happened yesterday there is also continuity. History, in other words, is a process of continuity in
discontinuity. History is also the way we are, it is the medium
of being human. It cannot therefore be something alien to God's
creation.

The study of history uncovers a pattern in the moments
and therefore tells the story of the continuity. One factor in the
continuity is the existence of the Church as a kind of concrete
embodiment or sacrament of the continuity of human history,
and in a special way of Christian history. God's gift of the Spirit
to the followers of Christ was the promise that they would constitute a community of life throughout history, preserving the
memory and re-presenting the presence of Jesus Christ. The
Spirit is what provides the permanence in change, by safeguarding the community which exists to keep the gospel intact, and
at the same time to re-present it to different generations. The
same two ideas are again those of permanence and change.
The community called "Church," we could say, guards history

itself against the ultimate fragmentation that would come about if this visible element or permanence in change ceased to exist.

In our confusion about the hermeneutical problem, therefore, it is right to look to the Church as the guardian of continuity. But it is also right to emphasize two other matters. Firstly, we are concerned with the Church as community, with the living organism that reproduces itself. And secondly we are talking about the permanence of the gospel in its changing presentation, not the permanence of one vision of the gospel to the despair of a changing world. Once again, then, we must ask about the choice of today's actions which we must make to represent with maximum effectiveness Jesus' way of being in the world. But even the Church cannot help there. The Church is nothing other than these same questioning pilgrims. We cannot predict or command that certain courses of action will be or are right, still less can we assume that yesterday's solutions are also answers for today. Moreover, shall we choose certain actions that we think or are told are re-presentative of Christ, and pronounce them right, or shall we choose certain actions that we think are right, and then defend the right to do and hold them in the name of Christ? And if we take the former option, what is our protection against abstract or theoretical standards, even if they are clothed in the language of the Bible? But if we choose the latter, how do we give our well-intentioned work a clear direction?

PRESUPPOSITION AND IDEOLOGY

All contemporary theologians, not just those who can be classed as "political," are aware of the difficulties raised for the interpretation of texts by the modern understanding of the influence of history. Human beings are born with all their human qualities and capacities in embryo, but there is no gainsaying the fact that the development of these individuals is in large part due to the influence of their environment. The prevailing assumptions of their times, of the culture of which they are a part, of their peer-group, and of their family and friends—all have a share in this environmental conditioning. The influence of the closer groups, such as the family, is more conscious but may in many respects be only a tinkering with larger-scale attitudes, since the family itself shares the outlook of its times. In general, we can say that the individual is to a large extent the product of the community.

It is a commonplace in the field of study which is often called "the history of ideas" that the unconscious presuppositions of a given moment in history are the greatest help in understanding the times. The word "presupposition" has to be used with circumspection, since it is too easy to assume that it is derogatory when it is not. We are not talking about *bias*, which is a kind of personal leaning toward one side or another of a given issue; thus, I might have a bias against women doctors or red-headed policemen. Of its nature, bias is irrational. Secondly, presupposition is not *prejudice*. Prejudice means having made up one's mind in advance of a fair appraisal of all the evidence in some particular matter. The classic example here is a racial or sexual prejudice, such that on any given issue I am inclined, for example, away from employing blacks or women or Jews or some other group. Once again it is irrational and may or may not be conscious.

Presupposition, like bias and prejudice, may be conscious or unconscious, but in itself it is neither good nor bad. Presuppositions are the framework of understanding in the mind of a given individual or the consciousness of a given culture. They are in other words things without which we cannot understand anything, unless we go back to the beginning of knowledge each time, and relearn everything. The laws of logic and of mathematics are the primary kinds of presuppositions, although even those can be culturally conditioned and may need revision, as Newton and Einstein and others have shown in their time. But although presuppositions can and must be reviewed by some of the people some of the time, although we should each of us try to avoid passing off our biases and presuppositions, we cannot always be scrutinizing the framework of our understanding. If we did that, we should never have time to understand anything but our understanding.

We can say, then, that presuppositions are inevitable, and that they are collectively the framework through which an individual or a culture interprets experience. If we think of *understanding* as the theoretical human capacity, then understanding through the lens of presupposition is the meaning of *interpretation*, or concrete historical understanding. So we return to the hermeneutical problem, although we now find it phrased a little differently: in the matter of reading the texts of the scriptures, it is a question of the relationship between the understanding of the world through the presuppositional lens of the first-century Palestinian Jew, and that of the twentieth-century person. Overcoming this hermeneutical "gap" involves, therefore, both an understanding of the presuppositions of the times in which the text was composed and an awareness of our own. We can reject neither without in so doing precluding the very possibility of genuine understanding.

The inescapability of presuppositions is often emphasized in political theology. There are many kinds of presuppositions, of course, and it is difficult to generalize about those which you and I would hold in common. Certainly, the more they lie in our collective cultural subconscious, the more influential they may be and the more harmful they could become. But those upon which the political theologians concentrate are not surprisingly the ones which can be seen as a product of socio-economic conditioning or political ideologies. To some extent these types of presuppositions are rather obvious and so might be thought to be less of a problem. Unfortunately they can often be reinforced by bias, prejudice, and self-interest.

The social class or the level of affluence of the group into which each of us is born clearly influences our view of the world. The more social advantages we have, the friendlier will be the face the world presents to us. Money and status open doors and take the chill off the wind. And, of course, the more comfortable we are in our world, the less inclined we shall be to make radical changes in its organization. It is true that many reformers and revolutionaries have come from socially-advantaged classes, but to become such a person involves a change of heart or conversion so that the individual looks upon the world from the position and often through the eyes of those to whom that same world seems anything but friendly and equitable. It involves changing presuppositions, or at least a conscious recognition and rejection of inherited assumptions, and a conscious effort to identify with a different vision of society.

One of the central issues raised by political theology is this matter of sets of presuppositions' influencing and even controlling one's outlook on the world. The central problem with the inherited presuppositions which we cannot help is that if they remain unexamined they can maintain or support an *ideology*. For our purposes we define an ideology as a systematic interpretation of and program for the world. It is usually both analytic and constructive. Its reading of history explains the present and dictates proposals for the future. It may be as conscious and concrete as Marxism or monetarism or capitalism, it may be as inchoate as a "conservative" or "liberal" outlook on the world. We may know that we espouse a particular ideology; we may not. Either way it is intimately involved with our inherited presuppositions and any critique must take account of those deeper assumptions.

IDEOLOGICAL SUSPICION

Our way of looking at the world may and perhaps must be influenced from the outset by unexamined presuppositions over which we may have limited control. The critical tool with which political theology proposes to confront this endemic social disease is the exercise of *ideological suspicion*. The term has a quasi-scientific ring which it does no harm at all to debunk just a little. It refers to the fact that any views we have, about anything at all, are inevitably conditioned to some extent by our upbringing, by the social class to which we belong, by the culture and age into which we have been born. The consequence of all this may be that however right-minded or idealistic we seek to be in our determination to represent Jesus Christ's way of being in the world, it is more than likely vitiated from the outset by the cultural perspective we assumed at our birth. We may seem at times to be trapped by history.

The recourse to ideological suspicion is a means to subject our view of the world to severe scrutiny. If we are broadly middle-class in our origins, how can we view the world as God's poor? If we are brought up in western Europe, how can we truly see the point of view of the impoverished masses of the third world? At one level, it is simply impossible; the perfect recourse of becoming God's poor or joining the suffering peoples of poor countries is not something readily open to most of us. But if the problem is insoluble, or the solution impossible, it may not be enough simply to acquiesce.

Ideological suspicion means examining our presuppositions, but it is not only with our view of the world that we are concerned. Engaging in political *theology*, we shall also have to ask about our view of God and of the relationship between God and the world. This application of ideological suspicion may be more difficult to accept. After all, we may think we receive our concept of God from the scriptures, perhaps mediated to us through the traditions and teaching of the Church. But if we apply our understanding of the hermeneutical problem to this thought, we will see how immensely complex the whole matter can be. As an interpreter, I have my presuppositions and perhaps my ideology. The world of the text of the Old Testament and that of the New each had its own outlook. Tradition and teaching are themselves a whole series of interpretations, every one bearing the marks of the minds and world of its time. In an endless series of historically conditioned attempts to understand, the elements of discontinuity threaten to crowd out those of continuity.

The problem can be illustrated with a simple example. Consider the biblical references to God as "king," and to the kingdom or reign of God. Then imagine how you might respond to these terms if you were a first-century Palestinian, a subject of Genghis Khan, or a citizen of a contemporary constitutional monarchy like Great Britain or the Netherlands. How very different might the responses to the words be!

The example generates a simple observation. We inherit such concepts in the Bible, and too frequently fail to subject them to any kind of historical understanding. Or we read texts in which the current cosmology made a two-tier universe perfectly acceptable, and we do not know where to start when it comes to dismantling the viable understanding of that time to replace it with one for our own.

Political theology makes use, then, of the notion of ideological suspicion. It asks for a critical approach to personal presuppositions, to the social and political assumptions of communities, and to the texts of scriptures and the worlds in which doctrinal pronouncements were enunciated. Ideological suspicion must be accompanied by *exegetical* suspicion. But we are also asked not to forget what has come to be called the problem of *false consciousness*. This is a simple idea: namely, if we examine presuppositions, of ourselves and of our times, of our Church or of our sacred writings, it must never be forgotten that you or I, the subject, the interpreter, is still working through at least some of those presuppositions.

The problem of false consciousness points to the inescapability of at least some presuppositions. Without them, understanding itself would not occur, unless such a thing as a completely ahistorical understanding were possible. But then we should never have needed interpretation in the first place, and the fundamentalists would have been right after all. The fact that understanding is always partial, always includes an element of uncertainty if not of misunderstanding, implies a hermeneutical gap even between you and me. You may feel that the gap is quite large at times, but, large or small, noticed or not, it is there. This gap, which is what makes the act of understanding as interpretation necessary, is also what makes the reappropriation of truth in a new world possible. It can never be enough simply to repeat the words of another time.

PRE-IDEOLOGICAL COMMITMENT

If at least some presuppositions are unavoidable, this does not mean that ideology cannot be side-stepped. Some theologians argue that is possible and even necessary; they propose a *pre-ideological commitment to the oppressed*—we may prefer to call it *a preferential option for the poor*. In political theology, theology "comes after," and the Christian life is the individual's expression of faith within a community, not in the first place by formal agreement to a set of beliefs, but in an instinctive response of commitment to the oppressed and outcast or *marginalized* in society. This response is modeled on the faith of Jesus, which was faith as a commitment out of obedience to God. Jesus sensed the nature of his mission or call from God and followed it to his death. This commitment to the will of his God was his faith. Consequently political theology argues that contemporary Christians must follow the same pattern. Following upon this identification with certain social groupings, which may involve a shift of perspective and an abandonment of certain presuppositions, the Christian comes to see the gospel in a different light.

Let us now take a closer look at the pre-ideological commitment. It sometimes seems as if the claim is that there is an instinctive (hence, pre-ideological) commitment to an immediately obvious class of socially oppressed people. In societies like those of most Latin American countries, this is perhaps realistic, though it is hard to see how any action escapes *all* traces of ideology. It becomes highly problematic, however, when the society in question is the relatively more complex Western kind of society, where the poor are still very much in evidence, but where the dividing line between rich and poor is harder to locate, and where there are more and sometimes more pressing kinds of marginalization than that of poverty—unemployment, imprisonment, mental illness, old age, racial prejudice. These categories identify distinct social groups whom the majority are happy to forget.

Despite these reservations about the term "pre-ideological commitment" as an expression of faith it does seem that political theology has drawn attention here to an important, even crucial insight. Fully human behavior is not behavior that has been dictated by a rational examination of the issues, but instinctive or unconsciously motivated behavior which on reflection is susceptible of a rational defense. When we act in this way we are responding to a situation as human beings, not as intellects alone, and although there is a danger that subsequent reflection may reveal we acted unwisely, yet if that later consideration justifies our acts, then we can with confidence dub what we did as "truly human." Our analysis of our action will reveal that it corresponded to what we believe to be true human nature. If we had stopped first to analyze the situation and deduce what would be the fully human thing to do, the moment would have slipped by, and an action taken under those conditions would be at least one-sidedly intellectual and open to all the harmful effects of abstraction and ideological bias that we have discussed above.

If this description of fully human action is accurate, then the liberation theologian's definition of faith as a pre-reflective commitment is fundamentally accurate. Faith is an attitude in which we find ourselves when we reflect upon what we take to be of absolute importance in our lives, not a code we establish *a priori* and out of which we measure what direction our human responses are permitted to take. Faith as a commitment is an attitude dictated by our humanity, not by formal doctrines to which we owe formal assent.

If political theologians insist on defining faith as pre-reflective commitment *to the oppressed*, then there is a danger that it is at least a little misleading. Surely faith is a pre-reflective commitment to God, or at least to the call of God upon us? This distinction is not negligible; God is unknown in self, although visible in Jesus Christ, but then one of the chief senses in which God is visible in Jesus is in Jesus' loving fidelity to his mission. But just as we tend to say that God is visible primarily in God's effects in the world and in the Son, Jesus Christ, so faith, even as a pre-reflective commitment, is faith first in the meaning of Jesus Christ as the way to God and as showing us our own way to that way. If Jesus called us all to share in the work of building the kingdom, then faith in Jesus as the way of God and faith in our own call are one and the same thing. Our pre-reflective commitment too is one of loving obedience to the task demanded of us. But that task is discovered in a call that rarely comes as a voice from heaven.

This faith as commitment to the call is expressed, as we have seen, through instinctive human responses to the world around us. Only later, theoretically at least, is this understood to be faith in the way of Jesus Christ. For some it is never understood in that way; some never receive the message of the gospel in so many words. But that does *not* negate the value of their activity in building up the kingdom, because that activity is human activity, the only kind of activity of which even Christians are capable. For those of us who call ourselves Christians, we are no better placed for being involved in the work of the kingdom, only better placed to understand what it is we are doing, and to know when we fail to do it.

The Christian, then, discovers the fully human work which

is his or her expression of faith by plunging into the world and its true needs, both spiritual and material. These come together under one rubric which is fundamentally Christian and yet acceptable to all people—namely, that what the world needs is the structure which makes it possible for all people to exercise their full humanity. They need to be free to be human. When the contemporary Christian becomes involved in a way of life which, directly or indirectly, is helping others to be more fully human—that is, when our lives take our own freedom and that of others seriously—then we naturally find our attention turning to the marginalized, to those in our own society whose freedom is under threat or restricted or denied. Then we are representing Christ in what we do. Praxis, in some ways, sidesteps the hermeneutical problem.

THE CHRISTIAN AND POLITICS

The question of the relation between abstract standards and a coherent direction becomes especially important in treating of more overtly political activity. Of course all actions which have a point of reference in the community are political, but some are consciously directed toward the creation of structures of freedom, and these can be more narrowly defined as political. This distinction goes some way toward answering the much-discussed question of how far Jesus himself could be considered a political figure. If we mean by politics a conscious program for organizing society in a certain way, and by a politician a person who operates upon such a program to bring it about as speedily as practicable, then of course Jesus was not a political figure. Yet it is quite certain that a good many of what seem to have been his basic attitudes had political implications. Jesus did not spend his life arguing for fundamental changes in social structures, but he lived in such a way that his life was a reproach, sometimes spoken and sometimes not, to those who justified themselves by filtering their lives to the last detail through a rigid interpretation of the law. He demanded a conversion or change of heart, asking people to judge their lives and their society through what they saw before their eyes, and then to interpret the law accordingly. If you are hungry on a day of rest, he said, you have the right to work to feed yourself, even though the law proscribes it. If someone is sick or needs help you must aid him, even on the Sabbath. A public sinner is no worse than a private hypocrite whose public life is apparently pure. The emotional and enthusiastic response of welcome of a known prostitute is worth more than the coldly formal politeness of a "good" man. God's love and mercy are needed more by the sinners and less fortunate, and benefit more those who recognize their need of them. How can we imagine that anyone who heeded Jesus' lessons and tried to follow his example would not find himself or herself adjusting his or her vision of society?

Just as our cosmology and our knowledge of evolution and astronomy and physics have changed totally since the time of Jesus, so has our awareness of political science. Consequently, the need to make Jesus' revolutionary message coherent in our times involves situating it in a politically conscious framework. It must be politicized. But this does not mean that it can or may be dressed in the terminology of any political ideology. It is quite impossible to give a particular political label to Jesus of Nazareth, because the lessons he taught were strategic rather than tactical. It was his inability or unwillingness to consider tactics which brought him to Calvary. But that tactical blunder was the triumph of the divine strategy at work in him. Just so, we shall expect to find in the actions of Christians today a clarity about the objectives of their sociopolitical activity and a conviction that the means they take to bring about those ends must be consonant with the values of the ends themselves. If, in other words, our aim is to bring about structures of freedom in which human beings can flourish, then what we do to fulfill this program must consist in acts which themselves express this human nature. This is the anthropological dimension of the eschatological reservation, the "already–not yet" of the kingdom. Just as the kingdom of God is with us now, but not fully, and salvation is now, but not in its totality, so the perfect freedom of human beings is inaugurated, and must therefore be acted upon. Acting upon it will help to bring it to its fullness.

All this dictates a form of eclecticism or pragmatism or opportunism in a Christian's attitudes to political parties. In the first place, the biggest mistake we can make is to take the well-trodden path of rejection of the two so-called extremes of communism and fascism because of some abstract denial of God or "the rights of the Church" which they are assumed to propound, then say that all political options which do not deny God (the remainder) are a matter of indifference. For Christians, no political party or program can be espoused totally non-critically, not even "Christian democracy." Following the party line or accepting a three-line whip is not something to which a Christian can ever give total commitment. The political objective of Christianity, which is the construction of concrete structures of human freedom, will always dictate a pragmatic stance and only relative commitment to this party or that, and sometimes to none at all, because of the relatively favorable opportunities to press the cause of justice. Christians in politics must therefore always stand critically toward the political status quo and be prepared to challenge current values and assumptions.

The relativism which a Christian brings to bear upon a given political program is not therefore apolitical, since it is based upon the concrete *existential* orientation of Jesus' life, with all its political implications. In consequence, the abstract denial of God is not the supreme crime in the eyes of a Christian; that is one reason why we are free to associate in our day-to-day social enterprises with members of all political and religious affiliations. It is the existential denial of God which has to be opposed—and this occurs whenever the freedom of human beings to be fully human is argued against or seriously trans-

66

gressed. It would be because and insofar as communism or fascism or capitalism did not follow the orientation of Jesus toward the empowerment of the marginalized to achieve their full humanity, rather than because of a denial of God, that it might have to be rejected. As it happens, in the past the Church has been too ready to accuse communism and too willing to accept fascism's defense of the rights of Church, family, and property at its own estimate. In today's world it is clearly not communism as such that is the enemy of Christianity or humanity, but belligerent nationalism of all kinds, with all forms of motivation, whether ideological or economic; the ideologically-panicky Soviet gerontocracy, greedy capitalism, neo-Nazism, Latin American "government of national security" (a form of fascism), grubby dictatorships like that of the Philippines, and the institutionalized oppression of South Africa are all to blame. In the face of the obstruction of human freedom which all these imply in their different ways, the abstract rights of the Church and the abstract denial of God are secondary matters.

5

The Circle of Understanding

THE TRUE MESSAGE OF POLITICAL THEOLOGY has to do with
the relationship between the world and the gospel. As Christians we all believe that the gospel has a message of hope for
the world, now as in the first days of Christianity. We probably
also agree with the claim that uncovering the word of God for
our time involves us in interpretation. We cannot simply take
Scripture as it comes to us. Nevertheless, the word of the scriptures also exercises a critical function toward the world; it is
at one and the same moment a message of hope and a word of
warning, calling Christians to *metanoia*, to personal reorien-
tation. This call to conversion urges Christians to achieve a
frame of mind in which the message of hope can be translated
into practical reality. The gospel hope is linked to a vision of the
kingdom of justice; but the vision seeks realization.

There is no doubt that in preaching the kingdom of God
Jesus was primarily addressing his message to the less fortunate
members of his society. His call was not addressed exclusively
to them, however; he also taught in the presence of the scribes
and Pharisees, met the powerful of his day, and ate in the house
of rich men and women. This contact with the more fortunate
did not lead him to modify or adulterate his claim upon the
hearts of his hearers. They heard the same message but being
different people it reached their ears in a different way. What
was heard by the blind and poor and the "sinners" as a promise
of a new scale of values and a proclamation of God's special
love for them was of necessity heard by the establishment as a
threat to a status quo which had served them personally very
well. Which way the wind is blowing is always relative to where
you are standing.

Political theology has a particular care for the place of the underprivileged and for the way in which they see the world. If the gospel is preaching a change of attitude, a transformation of personal and community values, a movement of reconciliation which will lead to the reign of God in history, then those who have less to lose will be more free to hear it. This is the *only* sense in which it is blessed to be poor. It would be wonderful if we all had more than enough and that this superfluity did not stop our hearing the truth of the world. But which wealthy person who was truly free of the wealth would not feel constrained in these days to give most of it away? And which of us in Europe and North America is not in some sense rich? The demand for a pre-ideological commitment to the oppressed, for all its impracticability and perhaps its impossibility, is inspired by a totally justified demand for us all to abandon those things which prevent our seeing the world as it really is. Only then will the gospel meet us as a word of unqualified hope and joy, and not as at least partially a painful censure.

Our understanding of the world affects our interpretation of the gospel. Conversely, the message of the gospel calls us to a particular understanding of the world. Human attachment to the world and to God struggle against one another throughout an individual's life, and this remains true (although more difficult to explain) when the individual is a believer in the incarnation, in which God and the world have irreversibly met. The conflict of the world and gospel is a *dialectical* conflict; the individual moves constantly between the two points, and interprets the one from the viewpoint of the other.

We know that our role in the world is to act on behalf of the reign of God. We have also seen that we must do this with more than half an eye on our own presuppositions, and we are familiar with the narrowness that the uncritical acceptance of an ideology entails. We are aware that our lives have both practical and theoretical dimensions; maintaining the right relationship between the two is of vital importance. The theory–

practice axis is a second dialectic to add to that of world gospel. In this second conflict our convictions give direction to our activity, and our actions illumine and authenticate our convictions. Thus, it encompasses the first dialectic, in the sense that what we believe about the relationship of world and gospel is assessed by the extent to which it is borne out in the lives we lead.

Our entire lives take place within the confines of the theory–practice dialectic. We can never go back to the beginning, wipe our minds and feelings clean of every historical bias and every theoretical judgment, and start with a *tabula rasa*. It cannot be done. Instead, we have to see our lives as a progressive training or purification of our activity in the world. Here where we stand in history is the starting-point, and the past is past. At the same time, being aware of the past and our role in it will make the beginning of understanding easier, and the possession of a sense of the direction in which we should move is our personal assurance that we have not completely lacked understanding so far.

This talk of understanding may sound as if we are putting some purely mental category in the highest place, and this would be unacceptable to the political theologian. We would rightly be accused of doing that if we were advocating purely theoretical understanding—the capacity of the intellect by which we can shuffle and re-arrange concepts. To set this up as our objective would be self-contradictory, since the point toward which the whole book leads is the claim that understanding the gospel can occur only when our understanding of the world is at least moving in the right direction, and this is achieved only by living in a certain way. The understanding with which we are concerned, therefore, is the practical understanding which comes from a living acquaintanceship. It is the difference between the theoretical "I know about" and the concrete "I know," or the knowledge of a person we have by reading a biography and the knowledge we have by living with the person. Christianity is never on the right lines until the relationship of the individual and the community to Jesus Christ is seen as knowledge rather than knowledge about.

In political theology, the process of understanding has acquired a high-sounding name: *the hermeneutical circle.* It is intended to suggest on the one hand that the process of understanding is circular, and on the other that in this circularity true understanding (interpretation) occurs. The hermeneutical circle, it is fair to say, is the heart of the method of political theology; because all true understanding is interpretation, I can never understand something as its writer wrote it, but I must bring my understanding to bear on it and uncover anew its truth in the here and now. It is the point at which theology becomes possible, because it is here that reflection begins. In theory, at least, it is chronologically subsequent to the pre-ideological commitment, and moves into action when, with my insight into the nature of the world sharpened by that commitment, I return to the gospel. What do I find there?

Juan Luis Segundo, one of the most influential of liberation theologians, argues strongly that true theology is marked by its partiality.[1] Academic or traditional theology is condemned for being abstract, for not being situated in some real-life context. Theology which is worth the name grows out of a particular historical situation, and therefore shares in the particular preoccupations of its time, its geographical location, and its cultural and socio-economic slot. Liberation theology, says Segundo, is just such a partial theology; it begins from a sociopolitical slant and is proud of it, not because it is biased but because the theologian's world is initially a purely human world. Human values come before theological acumen. Theology "comes after."

All liberation theologians, whether by birth or by conscious choice, ought to be identified with some marginalized constituency—blacks, Hispanics, women, Native Americans, and so on. There is no such thing as an academic liberation theologian, although there are academic theologians who study or know something about liberation theology. Every liberation theologian adopts a partial viewpoint, that of the group with which he or she identifies, not to exclude others but simply because such roots are essential to the enterprise. But they share a basic belief about theology—namely, that it is through reflection on the relation of experience and the gospel that God's saving word is uncovered as the will-to-liberation of the oppressed.

There is, of course, nothing inherently wonderful in being oppressed, and there is no guarantee in itself that such a situation will make your theology especially sound. However, being in such an oppressed situation stimulates the first of the two preconditions that Segundo identifies as necessary for true theology: namely, that the questions which arise out of reflection on the experience of the community are sufficiently fundamental. Segundo says that they must be so rich, basic, and general that they inevitably lead to a change in customary conceptions of the great existential and metaphysical preoccupations—life, death, knowledge, society, politics, and the world in general. The questions, in the terms we have used earlier, must be such that they will challenge our ideological presuppositions.

Identification with the oppressed destroys complacency, whether intellectual or existential. The comfortably bourgeois or relatively affluent Western theologian can at best make only an intellectual effort to understand the predicament of those far less fortunate. The theologian's situation does not of itself demand a change of attitude to the world; it remains friendly and comforting. But even a week on the streets of New York with empty pockets, artificial and limited as that might be, would be enough to show anyone that the ordered world so many of us take for granted is just one way of looking at something which is capable of appearing infinitely more sinister.

The second presupposition for a political theology is a change in our way of interpreting the scriptures, and this grows

out of the first. The argument of the political theologian is that
the prevailing interpretations of the scriptures have been dictated by the ecclesiastical and academic status quo. Consequently, the accepted reading is white, Western, middle-class,
and clerical. The current interpretation of the gospel therefore
reflects the assumptions of such people (that is, most of us) and
the ideology of the religious and even political establishment.
The change in interpretation of the gospel that is needed for a
political theology to emerge occurs naturally when the kind of
persons whose social situation has forced upon them a radical
revision of their way of looking at basic human problems comes
face to face again with the text of the scriptures. When we understand the world differently, we hear the gospel another way.

Segundo believes that these two preconditions lead to a
consideration of four decisive factors in the establishment of a
true hermeneutical circle. They are: that our way of experienc-
ing reality will lead us inevitably to ideological suspicion; that
the application of this ideological suspicion to the general super-
structure of ideology in the world, and to theology in particular,
will occur; that this in its turn will lead to exegetical suspicion,
where ideology critique is extended to the scriptures themselves;
and finally that a new hermeneutic, by which he means a new
way of interpreting the scriptures, will emerge. Without these
four factors the hermeneutical circle is not complete, and political theology is not possible. With them, the theological revolution is possible although there is no guaranteed success.

These four stages are obviously a stratification of the two
preconditions, emphasizing once again that the true starting-
point is experience of a particular way of life. However, it also
seems clear that the new interpretation of the gospel that one
hopes will appear can take up a critical stance toward the way
of life out of which it emerged. In other words, the circle is truly
a cyclic process.

When the new hermeneutic arises in the context of the
life-experience of this or that community, when the herme-

neutical circle is complete, then and only then is theology pos-sible. Life-experience and the scriptures stand in creative con-frontation, the one enlightening and being criticized by the other. In liberation theology, this has occurred in the context of the third world, and of various marginalized groups in first-world countries, notably in the United States. The gospel is no longer understood as an abstract document, but a word directed to a people with a history. The question now arises: what word does it address to *us* with *our* history?

NOTE

1. See *The Liberation of Theology* (Maryknoll: Orbis, 1976).

6

Doing Theology in Our Real World

PARTIALITY

IN THE FIRST PLACE, as the last chapter has demonstrated, our theology will be *partial*, dictated by our concerns and growing out of the experience of our own community in the United States of the 1980s. It may or may not be of use in some other community. That is not our concern; the universal truths of Christianity have been stated often enough, and there is no need to try once again to articulate them. Our task is both more modest and more urgent. It begins with the need to reflect on the nature and purpose of our society, and, armed with the fruits of that reflection, to turn to the scriptures. We shall need to listen for the word the gospel speaks to *us*. Whether it is a word for anyone else is not for us to say.

Partiality is a direct result of the Christian religion's incarnationalism. Jesus was the incarnation of God as man at a particular time in Palestine. Christian theology has succeeded in making him a figure of abstract truth, from which stem various theoretical christologies: liberal, kenotic, existentialist, revolutionary, or whatever. But if incarnation means anything at all it means that Jesus *as God* belongs with his history, and we do him an injustice if we tear him from that history and "apply" him to whatever we wish or wherever we happen to be. The task of christology is much harder; it is to see who and what he was in his time and for his time, and to teach Christians how to strive to be the same in and for theirs.

The Latin American experience is not our experience, although it has much to teach us. In many countries of Latin America essentially similar social situations exist. Large groups of peasants are oppressed, landless, poor, and illiterate, as a direct result of oligarchic social structures. Twelve families own most of the land in El Salvador, even after modest "land reform." The people themselves live a kind of contemporary realization of the crucifixion, and bring home that reality to the Church, which can do nothing but respond to the situation with which it is surrounded. When theologians reflect on the reality of El Salvador, what results is what we in North America call liberation theology. For them it is simply theology.

In our own communities, partiality will mean something different, but it will be the fruits of the same process of seeking out the voice of the crucified in our society and responding to it as best we can. As that society is more complex, so it may be harder to hear the authentic voice of the marginalized. There may be several voices: the cry of those who are the "wrong" color or race; the frustration of those who cannot find work; the speechless appeal of those who are locked away for life in mental-care institutions; the loneliness of the old; the helplessness of the truly poor; the pain of the abandoned, the divorced, the handicapped. Insofar as the very existence of these groups and their problems are a silent critique of our society, so the solutions which the gospel will call us to search for will themselves be political. They will be concerned with finding the social structures in which these various groups will be free to be fully human.

WHO DOES THEOLOGY?

There is a certain kind of romanticism which delights in declaring that theology is "the people's work." It is not the whole truth, but it is a half-truth; not to be dismissed, but possibly dangerous. After all, we should be laughed out of court if we announced that philosophy or biochemistry is the people's work, and there is an equally technical element in theology. At the same time, it is equally unsatisfactory to say that theology is "the theologian's work." Again it is a half-truth; it all depends on what you mean by "theologian." If it is meant to suggest, for example, that theology is the work only of those who teach theology in universities, or those who work in seminaries, or bishops, or clergymen, then it is simply not true. It may be the work of some or all of these people, but only if they are truly theologians, and this will demand their rooting in a concrete historical community and its experience.

If theology starts from reality and not from ideology, then a theologian is someone who also starts from reality rather than with a preconceived system. True theology is inductive. The first priority for the theologian is therefore to be in touch with reality; it is a necessary condition for doing theology. This in itself does not mean that he or she must be desperately poor, starving, or working in a factory. But it does mean that the world of the theologian must be one in which he or she is consistently and progressively seeking to free the self from the chains of all ideologies, religious or political or cultural.

The best cure for an ideology is the facts, through personal experience. Contact with ordinary people living ordinary lives has always been good medicine for the theoretician. Consequently, people whose service of the Church is primarily to engage in theological reflection absent themselves from day-to-day contact with the mass of the people at the peril of their service. Our theology can be uncovered and conducted, it would seem, only by those who are sufficiently in contact with reality that they can be purified of all forms of ideology. At the same time, contact with reality does not of itself free us from ideology. It also requires a measure of good common sense, intelligence, and humility before the facts.

In principle, theologizing is the birthright of every Christian. Theology in itself is not a complex activity; it really amounts to nothing more than reflecting on the interrelations of scripture, tradition, and contemporary experience. Clearly, anyone who reads the Bible or listens to a sermon is doing theology, if he or she is engaged in these things with sufficient attention. But we can go further to claim an important role for the Christian community. The professional theologian must belong in a specific community, and at least some of his or her reflections will mirror those of the community, since they will constitute part of the theologian's contemporary experience. At the same time, the activity of theology has to be conducted, by at least some people, on a scientific and rigorous footing. Scripture, tradition, and contemporary experience are none of them self-evidently one thing or another, but internally complex and needing analysis and explication. Consequently, however much we locate theology in the community, we cannot expect the community to reflect easily on what it may not fully understand. The role of the professional in that community is partially to advance the understanding by the community of the units which are used in theological reflection, and partially to learn from that same community's reflection.

The presumption of the academic or professional theologian is too often that everyday experience is secondary to theological acumen; that of the ordinary Christian may well be that political shrewdness, intuition, or plain common sense constitute a clear path to good theology. We have already said enough about the former assumption; it simply produces abstractions. But the latter is equally dangerous. Theology is not social work or community action done for the sake of the gospel; it is at least partially a rigorous mental discipline. If we are not learned in its ways, we should no more think that our theology is as good as that of Karl Rahner as we should imagine that our soufflé could match Escoffier's. However, the fact that we are not in the Rahner class should no more cause us to give up reflecting theologically than a collapsed soufflé should put us off frying omelettes for life.

The question of who does theology cannot be given a simple answer. The believing community is the locus of theology, which is to say that out of the community true theology arises, and that theology entirely divorced from either the experience or the concerns of the community is of no significance. But the professional theologian is a part of this believing community, and is rightly considered to hold a specialist role; he or she is the person whose gifts and learning equip him or her to articulate theological truth in full consciousness of its complexity. The theologian and the community need one another.

CONSTRUCTING THEOLOGY

Now that we have embraced the partiality of our theological vision, and have identified the community as its locus, we can turn to the concrete steps we need to take in its construction. This brings us again to the hermeneutical circle which we considered in the last chapter. Before we address that, there is the preliminary question of just what impels us into the hermeneutical circle. Pre-ideological commitments and preferential options have causes. The most satisfactory answer is that of Jon Sobrino,[1] that contemporary theology begins in *indignation*. It is in the indignant response to the cries of the suffering, or indignation in face of our helplessness to change that suffering, that we can find the strength to abandon ideological positions and listen to the gospel. In this we follow in the steps of the psalmists, the prophets, and Jesus himself.

The first step in building our theology is immersion in the everyday world. Reality is our starting-point. We said above that the believing community is the locus of theology. Now we have to add that the whole of everyday reality, the entire believing and non-believing society in which we live, is the reality with which the believing community itself must be in touch, and upon which it must base its reflections. The Church exists neither for God's sake nor for its own, but for the sake of the world, and perhaps it is a truer evangelism which brings others

81

the reality of their full humanity rather than proclaims a gospel which they are neither willing nor able to hear. In any case the believing community's existence for others is an obvious reflection on the fact that injustice is no less unjust, hunger no more bearable, when the sufferer is agnostic, atheist, or pagan.

Our twentieth-century world has an inescapable international dimension. We cannot separate ourselves from events on other continents, as our concentration on our local community may suggest. Nevertheless, our first duty is to be involved in the reality of our situation and to approach the reality of other parts of the world through our implication in the structures which contribute to it. Indignation on behalf of so-called underdeveloped nations (if it has not passed through analysis and appreciation of our "home" community) is just another and more sophisticated abstraction.

Being involved in the reality of our situation means, concretely, that if we stand apart from it, physically or mentally or emotionally, we cannot even begin to do theology. The theologian in particular must live in a way which will bring about progressively more freedom from the chains of all ideologies. It does not have to mean that abject poverty or social deprivation is a *sine qua non* of theological authenticity, but it is not clear how such a social situation would harm theology. More importantly, though, our situation must not set us apart from those who are deprived, and our mental attitudes must be a product of experience. It is perhaps a counsel of perfection, for those of us who have ears to hear. And many of us may turn out like the rich young man, even if our valued possessions are principally our pet theories.

If the Christian does succeed in being part of reality, taken up with the real world, the result is that he or she will no longer think in ideologies, but say the truth as it is found. Of course, we can never become complacent in our possession of the truth or our freedom from ideology. We have to proclaim the truth *now*, and then move on untrammeled by what we have said. The Christian thinker is in some ways a prophet, speaking a truth that may at times be only a voicing of the pain of the marginalized. When we make the mistake of grasping and holding on to the truth we have uttered, and maybe even beginning to turn it into a new ideology, we shall be close to trying to explain that pain away.

So the truth must be said and set free in the world, left to its own devices. It is not to be erected into a system to which labels can be attached. This is the reason Latin American theologians come to European conferences on liberation theology with a faintly embarrassed air. They do not want to be tied to a system. They simply wish to be free to speak the truth. And they rightly suspect our search for a new textbook. If you ask third-world theologians what we should do in our countries of Western Europe or in North America, they just smile and keep silent. They would not be so presumptuous.

The practical value of being in touch with reality is that the concepts of Christianity acquire content. Great books could be and have been written about the ideas of sin and repentance, tied to the notion of an "offense against God" or perhaps that of an offense against my neighbor or myself. But the presence to us of the dispossessed and marginalized, in our daily lives but also in magazines and on television, brings home to us that sin is anything which bears down upon and crucifies the people. Sin is just not in the acts of private individuals, but somehow woven into the fabric of society, built into its oppressive structures. Petty private acts of greed and power-hunger are one face of the coin, while the other is the callousness of power politics, aggressive economic colonialism, and the unwillingness to take responsibility for the global effects of political and economic policy. *Realpolitik* can be sinful.

The corollary of sinfulness is repentance. Here again repentance is most often taken to mean "feeling sorry for my sins," but this is dwarfed into insignificance when we come to realize that as citizens of our societies we are personally im-

83

plicated in systemic injustice. Macro-sin demands macro-repentance, and this amounts to expressing repentance in doing something about the structures of a society or a policy which crucifies others. This puts repentance on a much firmer footing than easy sorrow, and brings its own very practical penance. We move, to borrow Cardinal Newman's phrase, from notional to real assent when our everyday experience gives content to the abstractions of theological science or catechetics.

The most pernicious counter-influences encouraging Christians to leave social sin out of account are religious and not political ideologies. Foremost among these is the ideology of dualism, which pops up all over the place, but is more evident in some forms of Protestant fundamentalism and Lutheranism. We discussed this position at length in the first two chapters, but perhaps a brief reminder would be useful here. The crux of such views lies in a radical distinction between the realm of faith and the realm of works. Faith is part of the relationship between the individual and the God who freely chooses to justify that individual. This faith is in the saving sacrifice of Jesus, through whose blood God has justified sinners. Consequently, those individuals who are justified live in two worlds, that of faith (in a "vertical" relationship with God) and that of works (in a "horizontal" relationship to society). Of course, most reputable versions of this world-view require of the justified that they behave in the world as children of God, but there is no intrinsic connection between conduct in the world and status before God. It is therefore entirely possible to justify two sets of values for the two realms. The world has been radically secularized by being set apart from the divine dispensation, and exists not immorally but according to its own laws and by its own values. Government and justice are patterns of interrelated rights and duties, and no critique of or control upon the language of political priority and expediency is possible, necessary, or desirable. Any attempt to express a connection between political activity and salvation is met with utter incomprehension, not infrequently bolstered by the unenlight-ened self-interest of the wealthier portions of the white races who most often adhere to this world-view.

Traditional Catholicism also presents a set of overlapping dualisms. There is first and foremost the vision of this world as the training-ground for eternal life, which whatever else is said about it undoubtedly encourages political and social quietism. It is this view which blesses the poor because they will be rich hereafter. The second dualism is that of faith and morals. The former, as we have said at length in earlier chapters, is a matter of assenting to the rules of the Church as club, expressed in a series of venerable historical pronouncements and authoritative interpretations of Scripture. The second is a matter of assenting to similar rules for the conduct of individuals in their dealings with one another and with those outside the club. Salvation in this view is not simply an individual justification, but the reward of a paid-up subscription to the club. Both halves of the dualism are held together under the authority of the one Church, in which heresy is the ultimate crime and excommunication the capital punishment, now that burning at the stake no longer gets a good press.

The result of the Catholic position can often be surpris-ingly similar to that of its dualistic Protestant counterpart. This seems to me to be because of the idea of "separation of powers" which the Church grudgingly grew to accept over the centuries, but which in later years has proved so useful for assuring the continued existence of the Church in both fascist and commu-nist societies. This principle effectively requires the restriction of faith to the private domain (not unlike the two-kingdoms ap-proach mentioned above), and the focusing of morality upon private and particularly sexual conduct. Contraception and abortion are against the natural law, we are told, but what about the political programs which require large-scale unemployment in order to force down labor costs? This policy of co-existence, at its worst, leads once again to the idea that two sets of values, one for private and one for public life, are acceptable in a Christian. This is an extraordinary distortion: after all, the private conduct of the Christian is being modeled on the public life of Jesus!

Both Protestant and Catholic traditions, of course, can be read in ways which bolster rather than confront the close association of political life and social systems with the core of Christian belief. Protestantism has to shed its excessive individualism and its tendency to equate morals and conventions. Catholicism has to correct its inclination to see the Church as the one channel of salvation, and even to consider the preservation of the Church as an end in itself.

Political theology confronts such religious ideologies with ideological suspicion and with what is sometimes called ideology critique. It does not flatly deny that they contain any truth at all, arguing instead that the truth of their respective positions will become visible if the starting-point for theology and worldview is from the pattern of God's activity in human society here and now. Starting from reality, ever-changing as it is, calls for a constant process of modification. Changing human experience and growing understanding of that experience meet a more scientific reading of the scriptures.

SOCIAL ANALYSIS

If the first step for theology is to start with reality, the second is to analyze that reality. This is a direct consequence of the fact that historical understanding is of its nature always developing. The term "social analysis" may suggest something alarming, like a government committee of inquiry, a university department of sociology, or a political party propaganda machine. Essentially it should not be threatening; it is a matter of looking around and trying to understand our experience, in order to respond in a constructive fashion. Once again, this needs to be done without the use of systemic preconceptions or ideologies. For this reason, social analysis follows upon immersion in human everyday life and does not precede it or impose upon it.

Because ideological presuppositions can dictate the results of social analysis, sociologists are no more above suspicion than are academic theologians. They too need at least one foot in the community they examine, and not only on a field-trip with clipboard in hand. Similarly, if the locus of theology is the believing community, although there may be specialists in theological reflection to aid that process, so the locus of social analysis is the society itself, although again with the help of the professional. Even "society" is an abstraction, however; what we mean is *this* or *that* society. And nothing is more theoretical than much sociology. A way has to be found to make the social analysis as concrete as possible.

In this need for realistic social analysis, the grassroots community is particularly important. This kind of analysis is not interested in the first place in how what is happening in Belfast or New York City or Amsterdam fits into the pattern of Irish or American or Dutch society, still less how it confirms or fails to confirm a particular hypothesis. It wants to know what is happening on the spot, how people are feeling, and how they are reacting to their experience. "What is to be done" is always first some plan of action for that particular community; only later for extrapolation to a larger or different context.

The social analysis must also be a natural outgrowth of the indignation that arises in the believer from the experience of the grassroots community in the 1980s. Professionals can help: the members of the community must do the analysis. It is their experience that is under analysis, and the first purpose is to understand their own situation so that action may follow.

There is an exception to this emphasis on grassroots analysis. We not only need to know our own situation in order to understand it; we also need to know about the structure of the experience and events which brought us to this situation. We need, in other words, a social history of the community, both of the internal growth of our society and of our place in world affairs. In the United States such a project has been attempted as part of the Theology in the Americas program.[2] This is no easier to effect without the taint of ideology than any other matter, but the attempt has to be made. The American history describes the country's past and present in terms of infancy, adolescence, and maturity. Such historical working-papers are preconditions of becoming subjects rather than objects of national history, understanding it before taking control, and shaping that history toward selected ends. It is indispensable for a theology grounded in contemporary reality to know about the origins of that reality.

MEETING THE SCRIPTURES

When immersion in reality has been informed by a social and historical analysis of American society, the moment of the third step has arrived. The believing community, guided by its experts, must now turn its attention to re-reading the scriptures. We should not forget the point we shall have reached in the theological process. We will have opted for partiality, and our immersion in reality will have brought us into contact with the injustice and oppression of our own society toward sectors of its own people. An informed awareness of the wider world will have awakened us to the ethical dimension of our country's international profile. We shall have been sensitized and conscientized, and we shall be ready to hear the gospel afresh.

In such a frame of mind, we should expect what strikes us in hearing the gospels to be as partial as the standpoint we have elected to take. Some matters will no longer have much impact upon us, because they do not speak to our experience, but other things will hit us hard, as if heard for the first time. One evangelist rather than another may have an impact on us. There is nothing wrong about that—the gospels were originally produced for particular communities at specific times in their history, and spoke to their needs and to the ways in which they needed to be challenged. Consequently, whichever community of the early Church is the one toward which we most approximate may well have a gospel which seems to us most apposite. My personal wager would be that Mark and Luke will seem more contemporary than Matthew and John, but which gospel in itself is not important.

A good example of how this partiality occurs can be found in José Miranda's book, *Marx and the Bible*.[3] When Miranda worked in Mexico after his theological training in Europe, one question came to overshadow all others: "How was it possible that Christian doctrine defended a private ownership of the means of production?" The question, or the name of Marx in the title of the book, are not of themselves significant in our context. The important point is that Miranda took his question with him to his reading of the scriptures. This is what he says about his method: "I will not attempt to find parallels between the Bible and Marx, but rather simply to understand the Bible. Our method will be the most rigorous and scientific exegesis."[4] In the late twentieth century, this is the only method we can adopt in reading the Bible; we cannot simply sit in a circle piously reflecting, or at a desk with a pen, mining the text for morals. Our listening has itself to be scientific, understanding the text for what it is, and bringing to its study all the methods of biblical exegesis on the one hand, and the tool of ideology critique on the other.

Following Miranda's example, we take the demanding questions that arise from our everyday experience with us as we do this contemporary listening to the scriptures. In consequence the things which will stand out will be those which speak to the question or questions which concern us. We should also be aware of the power of the gospel to point out questions which have not been adverted to. The power of the gospel to challenge its hearers cannot be neglected, and this power may be directed not simply at our presumptions and fixed ideas, but at the potential for growth which lies in the individual and the community subconscious.

The strands of the gospel which will undoubtedly stand out with a new clarity are the figure of the liberator God, who frees the people from one form of enslavement or another; the prophetic denunciation of idolatry and materialism; Jesus' orientation toward the poor, oppressed, and "marginalized" of his society; and the image of the "poor in spirit" as the chosen community. These matters will strike us because they resonate with our newly-awakened experience. Other things will fall into the background: the image of God as king, the more "supernatural" and apocalyptic of events and language, and the miracle stories. But the fact that they fall into the background involves no judgment that they do not matter. Partiality dictates acceptance of what is important to our experience, but does not license rejection of what does not seem crucial in this time and place. It may have had its time or be awaiting it.

Just as some themes may strike us freshly, so we may encounter certain figures in the Bible with whom we find ourselves identifying, even when this identification works to our discomfort. An obvious example would be the sad figure of the "rich young man," who genuinely wanted to know the way to perfection but was unwilling to pay the price when it was disclosed to him. Each day our newspapers carry stories of our inhumanity to one another. Every day we pass them over in apathy or unwillingness or inability to do anything about them. This brings us close to the heart of decadence. The voice of God is speaking through the poor of the world as clearly as it ever did in the past on the lips of the prophets, and our refusal to read the statistics and draw the conclusions is a form of refusing God. If, however, we find the courage to live in the real world with our eyes open, then the juxtaposition of that world and the New Testament account we have just referred to could be fruitful indeed.

When the world is confronted by the gospel, the gospel text itself is given the power to speak the language of the twentieth century. Of course, the text always has power to challenge us, but its impact is at its greatest when the hearer, who is the interpreter of what he or she hears, is sensitized by concrete experience of the real world and thus enabled to articulate the meaning of the gospel for today. We shall see more of this in the next chapter of the book, but even now it must be apparent that the possession of informed awareness and hard experience of the world will make it easier to identify that rich young man. He is all or most of us.

In this transforming juxtaposition of experience and text, the fourth and final step in doing theology is reached. Theology appears out of the effect of Scripture upon our sensitized consciences. In this process there are two important factors at work, well-illustrated in the parable of the sheep and the goats in chapter twenty-five of Matthew's Gospel. In the first place, it is insofar as we have found it possible to identify with the unfortunate and marginalized of the world that we shall hear God's words and see Christ's way as a comfort to us and an inspiration to struggle for just these groups of people. But the second point follows naturally from this: it is insofar as we personally find ourselves guiltily fortunate or our society privileged beyond what is just that we shall hear that same gospel as a warning and even as a condemnation.

This second element of material good fortune is present in the lives of the vast majority of first-world citizens, at least relative to the majority of the "have-nots." It is not a state of affairs that most of us can or even should alter overnight. Nevertheless, it is probably true to say that our way to salvation con-

91

sists in striving toward the kind of life in which the gospel is comfort and inspiration rather than condemnation. Caught between the two, blessed are we if we hear it even as a challenge.

NOTES

1. In a private conversation, April 1981.
2. Joe Holland, *The American Journey: A Theology in the Americas Working Paper* (New York: IDOC, 1976).
3. (Maryknoll: Orbis, 1974).
4. Ibid., p. xvii.

7

A Political Theology

ALL ACTS OF INTERPRETATION are a form of conversation between the interpreter and the text. The creative interaction
between the two out of which the interpretation is to arise can
be understood as a process of question and answer in which
both text *and* interpreter alternately challenge and respond to
one another. The juxtaposition of the politically sensitive Christian and the gospel text (by which I mean the whole corpus of
the scriptures as they contribute to the proclamation of the
good news) produces at best both a political Christian who is
alive to the demands of the gospel and a gospel interpretation
whose contemporary political significance has been brought
into focus. Reflection on this produces a political theology in
all its concreteness and partiality: concrete, because it relates
to a particular society in its demands for praxis; partial because
it does not necessarily apply in exactly this reading to any other
society, still less to other periods of history.

The shape of this concrete and partial political theology
reflects the concerns of a particular community, and the orientation to praxis which the gospel demands then and there. And
since the theology has to be the creation of that particular community, or it is nothing at all, it can never be laid down in all its
specificity in a book. To do that would be to invite the impo-
sition of yet another new theory upon a situation out of which
it did not emerge, and to whose questions it was not directed.
Nevertheless the principles of that theology, which will have to
take their final shape according to the local needs, can be stated
and have in most cases already been expressed (at least implicitly) in the course of this book. In this chapter I propose to

draw these principles together. I do not wish to argue that those I shall discuss here exhaust the list, but I think that they are all important and that they have grown out of reflection on Christian praxis.

FREEDOM FROM IDEOLOGY

The first principle is on every page of this book. Ideology, by which is meant here the conscious or unconscious espousal of a theoretical view of the world through which experience is filtered, whether it is political or religious ideology, distorts the gospel. However well-meaning the advocate of the ideology, it cannot but result in a certain rigidity of viewpoint at best, and a definite hardness of heart at worst.

It may seem strange to find political theology proposing an axiomatic distancing from political ideologies. Certainly, the principle leaves its proponents open to sniping from both right and left. The right wing of theology and of the Church in general is only too willing to praise theological opinion which seems to stand apart from the presumed atheistic horrors of Marxism or communism, but it is unhappy with the extension of the anti-ideological stance to include religious world-views imposed upon rather than growing out of experience. The left, on the other hand, is cheering from the barricades as the political theologian discards ecclesiastical triumphalism, but muttering darkly about "reformism" and "bourgeois tinkering" when it realizes that this does not necessarily involve opening the canonization process on Karl Marx.

The corrective to both extremes is simple; just as experience is held to replace abstract theorizing in theology, so experience must also dictate the political tools to be utilized toward the one end of the struggle for the reign of justice in the world. The theology of the kingdom grows out of the relations of experience and the gospels, as we have recently said at some length. The means to its inauguration are at least partially political. Consequently the attitude of the political Christian to political ideologies is relativist and thoroughly pragmatic. It has been argued frequently that in Latin America the Marxists are simply using the Church and its influence to further their own ends. This may sometimes be the case. However, it would be a mistake to assume that the ends of Marxists and Christians never coincide. Moreover, it is at least equally true that the Church is using the Marxists, because in some societies Marxism happens to be the most effective means toward the creation of concrete structures of freedom. As long as it remains the best local articulation of the political language for the liberation of God's poor, it will be valuable in the struggle for the kingdom. The moment it is no longer valuable—where, for example, as in the Soviet Union, the demonic element has triumphed—it must be discarded.

In discussing Jesus' political standpoint, we made a distinction between strategy and tactics. The political Christian is a strategic idealist and a tactical opportunist, but opportunism as it addresses the means to the objective cannot be entirely unrestricted. The end to be achieved dictates the means which may be used to bring it about. In other words, if the aim is God's kingdom of justice, the path toward it must be one of anticipating now the values which will reach their fullness of expression in the society which we are seeking to build. The end can never justify the means.

If the end can never justify the means, what are we to say about violence and violent revolution? Can violence ever be justified to bring about the kingdom? There is an immediate danger of giving glib theoretical answers to questions which arise from situations of which we have no direct experience. The justifiability of violence can be measured only from within the situation which may seem to call for it. Certainly, in those deeply unjust societies it may seem that what is called for is *counter*-violence in self-defense against the institutionalized violence of repressive societies. Take, for example, the two "repressive" societies of Somoza's Nicaragua and Ulster. In the former, Church and Christian communities gave their blessing to and participated in a violent struggle, while in the latter they have not to date done so. It is probable that both communities have come to equally correct conclusions in their different situations. Nevertheless, it seems to me a mistake to classify violence as a political weapon: rather, it is the desperate recognition that political methods have failed. It is a last resort. It is a clear example to the Church that morality may sometimes mean choosing the lesser of two evils—a lesson which could be useful in other areas of the Church's public witness.

INDIGNATION

The principle that true theology in today's world begins with indignation has also been touched upon before. It was derived from the experience of Jon Sobrino in El Salvador, and stems from direct and ordinary human experience of a social situation radically different from that prevailing in most "developed" nations. The indignation which we may experience in reading the gospel passion-narratives may be real enough, but it is a luxury when compared with the crucifixion of whole societies in our world. El Salvador is currently a crucified country. The people of the Bahai faith in Iran have been killed in large numbers because of their religious identity. The Afghans and the Namibians and the Palestinians and the Poles and the people of Northern Ireland and the primitive tribes of the Amazon basin all share the cry "My God, my God, why have you forsaken me?"

Indignation is of course an instinctive reaction to a state of affairs, and always precedes action. Sometimes the correct action is most likely to result if the indignation has time to cool.

But indignation can itself be a holy thing. Precisely because it is instinctive, and especially when it is other-centered, as the indignation of the middle-class Westerner must be if it is not to be simply laughable, it is an utterly human reaching out to and empathy with the suffering.

A problem with indignation is that all too often it never reaches the state of action. I can mute my indignation by claiming that there is nothing I can do, or assuage it by putting a small sum in the collection box or writing a check for CARE. Given the capacity for indignation, then, the important factor seems to be the proximity of that which has occasioned the indignation. The closest events are those which affect me personally, the next those which impinge on my family and friends, and so on. The brutal truth is that 6,000 killed in floods in Bangladesh roughly equals (in terms of impact) a hundred dying in a plane crash at the local airport, and that is overshadowed by the man next door slipping on a patch of ice and breaking his leg. And if I have a toothache . . . !

The recent depression/recession in the United States economy, continuing economic uncertainty, anxiety about the federal deficit, and so on have the merit at least of drawing our attention to recognizable social evils. For some of us, they have led to unemployment, itself a form of inclusion in the ranks of the marginalized. If the worst-case scenario for the outcome of current fiscal and economic policies should come to pass, many more of us may learn to empathize with the disadvantaged. This is not a matter for rejoicing, yet it may be necessary before indignation can truly come to pass. Knowledge of the realities of other people's plight must precede indignation. We cannot be indignant about that of which we are ignorant, and we cannot manufacture indignation at the behest of this or that theory of society. Indignation is a genuine human response to the experience of injustice. To be sheltered from the experience and thus precluded from feeling the indignation is itself a form of oppression. Freedom from this very subtle form of oppression comes only with the reshaping of the community to allow for suffering—with the indignation—with the subjects of more concrete oppression.

SUBJECTS OR VICTIMS OF HISTORY?

An experientially-based theology which is in part powered by a righteous indignation in solidarity with the oppressed proceeds naturally to radical liberative praxis. The gospel message of freedom is interpreted as the call of the creator–liberator God to realize the concrete structures of freedom in which all human beings will finally be free to hear the gospel message.

Everyone hears the gospel as in some sense a message of freedom. But the proclamation of our freedom is only a part of that message, and an inadequate one. As a word addressed to a people in history, it is also a call to build freedom, a call to liberation. The ability to hear it in this dynamic sense comes with our sensitization to the oppressive, life-denying structures of history.

How we hear the gospel message of freedom is a function, therefore, of who and where we are. The message received by the unregenerate bourgeois translates into a self-congratulatory "I thank you, God, that I am not as other men." The poor peasant of Guatemala is inspired by the gospel to fight for a freedom that is not yet possessed. The bourgeois who has at least begun to hear the call to *metanoia*, to change of heart, is both frightened by the threat of change and enticed by the vision of a society of justice which has stirred something deep within.

The respectable Christian citizen of first-world society must first undergo a personal revolution, a true Christian conversion. In some ways this relativization of one's own preconceptions about rights to living standards and unrestricted freedoms is a more difficult step to take than the peasant's adoption of arms to fight the forces of oppression. It endangers the body less, but the price of failure is exacted upon the spirit. Moreover, it involves a sensitivity to less obvious phenomena than one's own starvation or the early death of one's children. It requires above all else the recognition of the gospel call as a call to let go, to relinquish the center to the needy, to marginalize oneself and one's own concerns, to release the world from the grip of a bourgeois materialism, capitalist and sometimes even communist, which has succeeded in marginalizing two-thirds of the world's inhabitants, and even all those within the "developed" nations who do not or cannot hold the center—the unemployed, the old, the chronically sick, the mentally and physically handicapped, the imprisoned, and those whose actions or views threaten the status quo of materialism and acquisitiveness.

This translates into a political praxis which puts the rights of the various categories of the marginalized within the state in the first place, and those of the infinitely larger groups of marginalized people or nations in a similar position in the foreign policy of the political unit. It is quite obvious, of course, that nowhere in the world is there a nation so single-mindedly pursuing such a radical policy of self-abnegation. Such a step would certainly be classified as a form of political and economic suicide.

Fortunately, the principal and immediate focus of the believing community's liberative praxis is within its own grass-roots community. Here, the chances of doing something to implement concrete structures of freedom are much greater, but the subtle pressure not to do so is correspondingly high, since the cost of action is immediately felt. It is frequently more attractive to identify with political pressure groups which operate on a wider and more distant front, but they are all too often intensely theoretical. It is not that they have no usefulness, but that what use they have has to stem from the praxis of those engaged in them. That praxis and experience at the local level are consequently first in importance, at least chronologically.

Sometimes, chance, fate, or the forces of history can lead to *metanoia*. Adversity offers all of us the chance to grow. For this reason, economic recession or depression can represent a greater opportunity as (for a time) we are made more aware of how history can victimize us, and this holds out to us the chance of becoming more receptive to those whom history seems always to have singled out for harsh treatment. One of the greatest disservices that riches or security do to an individual is to hide the essentially fragile nature of life. Recession can of course itself be the cause of further oppression, as the rich nations climb to renewed prosperity on the backs of those whose fate it seems to be to remain eternally disadvantaged. In times of recession the word goes out to cut foreign aid and impose duties on "cheap foreign imports." This is simply a further consolidation of institutionalized oppression. Maybe we should hope for an economic crisis of such magnitude that recovery would not come so smoothly, though if the gap between North and South continues to grow, it will come without our having to pray for it. What will our instinct be then—protection or a thorough revaluation?

Another way to address the issue of advantaged and disadvantaged is to talk of subjects and objects of history. Those people are subjects of their history who have seized political activity as the process of building society. Those are and remain objects who consider that politics has to do only with the governing of society by an isolated, even if democratically elected, group within it. This distinction has nothing essentially to do with capitalistic or communistic, democratic or oppressive societies. In El Salvador peasant groups and the Church in general have laid claim to subjecthood, though they remain oppressed. In Britain or France or the United States the many millions who consider that their freedom and their political responsibility are expressed in the exercise of their voting rights remain for the most part objects of their history. They are, in their way, victims of their own democratic political structures. It is possible though not easy to write a theology of revolution; but no one can compose a theological justification for apathy or indifference.

From this perspective, the gospel call to freedom is a call to assume the dignity and responsibility of subjecthood, to step from passive enjoyment of freedom to active creation of a fuller freedom. The individual, always in the context of the group, is to be part of the mobilization of the believing community to create a society of justice and freedom to be fully human. Career politicians will not usher in the kingdom of God.

"Freedom to be fully human" is a phrase that should recall us to the demands of a specifically Christian anthropology. At the same time we need to act on the principle that the po litical tactics of Christians should be proleptic of the end to be achieved, the values of the reign of God in history. These two dimensions of our political theology, in association with the needs of our particular society, provide the criteria for the selection of concrete political objectives. As we pursue these objectives we simultaneously proclaim our rights to be subjects of our history, and this coming to subjecthood of the marginalized (even the comfortably marginalized citizens of the bourgeois democracies) *is* the inbreaking of the kingdom.

Concrete theological proposals, orienting the praxis of the grassroots community, will be discovered when within a given community the natural leadership is marginalized, even marginalizes itself, grants itself the status of listener, and relinquishes the center-stage to the spokespeople of the dispossessed. Obviously, a consequence of this will be that the political options the community will take up will be those which articulate the grievances of the oppressed—whether the cry of the un-

101

employed for the right to a job, the appeal of the homeless for a place to call their own, or the demand of this or that minority for a fair hearing. To make such matters the political priorities of the community is probably simultaneously to preclude the possibility of political power outside of a truly revolutionary context. Paradoxically enough, it may be in the free democracies that Christian political activity will always be marginal, usually be dismissed as idealistic, and frequently be genuinely subversive.

What of the issue of reform versus revolution? Political theology certainly advocates a revolution in the sense of demanding a total and systematic reversal of the normal order of political priorities. But the greater part of effective political theology has been developed in societies which are either in revolt or closer to revolution than our own. They are frequently scornful of mere reformism, often rightly seeing it as a palliative offered in order to preserve the peace for the sake of the status quo. Nevertheless, the means by which a genuine revolution of priorities or political consciousness are to be achieved must vary from one context to another. The war which was fought in Nicaragua, in its final stages even with the blessing of the institutional Church, was an appropriate means to a just society. This does not mean that it would be right to pursue such a course of action in any and every situation. Some societies offer more scope for peaceful development and others are so overwhelmingly oppressive that no violent revolution would at the moment stand a chance of success (for example, South Africa, the Soviet Union, and Haiti). But all societies, even the liberal democracies of Europe and North America, will fight with unimaginable ferocity when they come to realize, as finally they must, that the implications of a Christian political theology involve the end of the present socio-economic order. Democratic political structures need not and should not disappear. To this extent we are reformist and not revolutionary. But the inequities of the global economy which these same democratic societies tyrannously impose on the rest of the world must die or be destroyed before we can talk of justice. In this sense, Christians are true revolutionaries.

THE CROSS

Then Jesus told his disciples, "If any man would come after me, let him deny himself and take up his cross and follow me"
[Matt. 16:24].

Every life, even that of the most comfortable and affluent citizens of the world, is open to suffering. Everyone has his or her responsibilities, burden, and challenge. Through the courageous carrying of the cross everyone will be saved. And for rich and poor alike, the temptation is the same: to shirk the responsibility, to avoid the challenge, to leave the burden lying on the ground.

The surface existence which constitutes the life of the person who seeks to live within the easy cocoon of ego-centrism is characterized by Dorothee Soelle as "death by bread alone."[1] It encompasses the gross materialism of the affluent nations and the far more understandable cowardice of the peasant who prefers hunger to violent death. Soelle has also called attention to two tendencies within Christian spirituality which can reinforce this surrender to the forces of history—apathy and masochism.

Christian apathy is a form of social quietism often bolstered by the misapplication of texts like "Blessed are the poor in spirit." Christian masochism is the Calvinistic glorying in suffering as God's righteous punishment of sinners for their sinfulness. Both strands encourage passivity in the face of suffering and consequently impede or even obstruct entirely any attempts to identify the causes of suffering or to work for its amelioration or eradication. The consequences of apathy and masochism may therefore seem to be an extreme form of a tendency always present in any recourse to the cross. And yet the cross figures largely in political and liberation theology, not least because crucifixion is the condition of many societies in which it is most vigorous.

The cross is a symbol for the presence of suffering in all human lives. The suffering itself is a reality, not a symbol, and the symbol in its turn acquires its force from the reality of the suffering in the life of one particular historical individual. The symbol can therefore be seen to forge a link between the suffering of Jesus and the suffering of the contemporary human being. Our suffering, if it is to be interpreted through the symbol of the cross, has to be understood by first understanding the suffering of Jesus. And understanding his suffering means comprehending it both as the suffering of this particular man, and as the suffering of God.

In chapter two we discussed the way in which God was in history in Jesus Christ. The values which Jesus expressed in his life are validated absolutely as *human* values by the fact that they are the values by which God lived in history. In a similar fashion, the inescapability of suffering and death are proclaimed for us in the crucifixion of Jesus, but because of who Jesus is, Calvary also expresses God's involvement in and solidarity with the human condition in all its finitude. The death of Jesus is also the death of God.

God is not dead on the cross as a demonic glorification of suffering and negativity, however, but as a statement about the crucifixion and death of Jesus. Had he lived differently, he would not have come to this end; but had he lived differently, he would not have been the presence of God in history. The crucifixion has something to say about both the meaninglessness and the meaning of suffering. On the one hand, in even the most meaningless suffering, God is there. On the other, the suffering which has meaning is that which the world imposes on the one who wishes to bring about the kingdom of justice and peace. The cross is the clearest possible witness that God is subject to suffering, not for its own sake, but because some suffering is an inescapable part of being human, and because God suffers with humanity wherever the powers of this world sense the subversive presence of the kingdom.

BASIC COMMUNITY

Underlying all that we have said is a model of the Church. Political theology dictates a particular ecclesiological perspective. No human being is properly understood in isolation from the community, and no Christian makes sense, or has the strength to be a Christian, totally apart from the fellowship of other believers. This is not a theological principle so much as a basic human truth. The individual exists only because of the activity of a community, is born into and lives within a particular social network, and is alone really only at the moment of death, when even then the community offers what support it can and celebrates the passage of the individual from its presence. This involvement in the community is a political truth too, and consequently axiomatic in political theology which, as we noted earlier, is suspicious of the individualistic attitude to religion prevalent in some streams of Christian tradition.

Political theology is then even more ecclesiologically than anthropologically based, although that is perhaps to ignore the fact that the anthropology of political theology is anti-individualistic. The praxis which in principle gives rise to theology is a solidarity with the community of the oppressed. The theological reflection is in principle the reflection of the community, perhaps articulated by those whose status as theologians depends on their contact with the community. The focus of God's loving concern for the Church is consequently seen in the practical love of human beings in the visible community before it is felt channeled downward through an institutional hierarchy. The Church is the servant of the church, which is in turn servant of the world.

The Latin American social reality has led to the phenomenon of basic Christian communities or "grassroots communities" in which the challenge to social problems and institutionalized oppression goes along with reflection on the gospel and worship of the God who brings hope to the hopeless. The communities are not so much anti-church or anti-institutional as too busy with the praxis of the Christian life to be concerned with the theoretical posturings of a theology not derived from their experience or to understand the priorities of other Christian communities in other parts of the world. The involvement of such communities in social reform and revolution has of course brought them into sharpest conflict with the more conservative elements in their own churches and with the increasingly conservative administration of CELAM, the Latin American Bishops' Conference. In Medellín in 1968 it was CELAM which gave the first and firmest push to the development of liberation theology, but since then its work has been damped down by manipulation and pressure.

In "developed" nations the basic communities do not by and large exist. Nor is it entirely clear what form they would take; their character in Latin America is at least partially dictated by the very great shortage of priests and by the overwhelming importance of Christian communities as frequently the only organizations recognizing, protecting, and developing human rights. Within democratic societies there are many organizations of such character, and consequently no clear identification of the church-based communities as protectors of the rights of the oppressed. It may often be easier to obtain redress of at least some grievances by direct recourse to political measures. Moreover, the decline in the numbers of priests is nothing like the Latin American problem, and the community left without a priest is nothing like so economically and socially defenseless as the isolated rural village of Brazil or Central America. For all these and more reasons, basic Christian community may need to be as "local" in character as the theology which gives birth to it.

In the German social context, Johann Baptist Metz has identified three conflicting images of the Church, which he names a people's church, a bourgeois church, and a basic community church. His point is that the traditional model of the church as a paternalistic society has to some extent given way to a bourgeois conception of the church as supplying services to people who patronize it, and that that in its turn must give way to a "postbourgeois" church which can take initiatives:

> This threefold division accorded to images of the church corresponds, moreover, to the three types of theology dominant among us. First, there is a classical theology, which is fundamentally shaped by neoscholastic positions, and with a strong apologetic orientation on behalf of a people's, i.e., paternalistic church looking after the people. Next we have the beginnings of a bourgeois liberal theology which finds its church support in that process whereby Catholic Christianity in our country is itself increasingly taking on the form of bourgeois religion. This theology criticizes both the theory and praxis of church authority, and does this pre-eminently according to the standard of bourgeois freedom. Finally, there are the political theologians of liberation which bring into organic unity a productive critique of both church and society, aiming toward a basic-community church as "Church of the people."[2]

The major current critique of German political theology, even that of Metz and Moltmann, who are obviously influenced by the praxis of Latin American theology of liberation, is that their analysis has not been accompanied by praxis. It is certainly true that the existence of the paternalistic church and the bourgeois church are not matched by any very evident basic community church. But in the German reality we could not look for a workers', still less a peasants', church. Even the basic community church itself would have to be bourgeois to the extent that it would draw most of its people from the middle classes. How can you have a people's church (meaning a church of the poor majority of urban and rural workers) when the working classes are only minimally represented in most institutional religion in western Europe? How can you have a church of the oppressed when there is no focused sense of oppression?

Metz's classification can be applied with a little modification to the American situation. The old paternalistic model played its part for centuries in which first the sense of community and later the sense of ghetto bound people strongly to their local church, and in which believers were on the whole ill-educated and consequently unfitted to take responsibility for their church. Then the pastor was truly a "shepherd of souls." However, the last half-century has been marked by the dissolution of the local community and new emphasis on the family unit, and a general rise in the level of education of the Catholic laity accompanied, for better or worse, by the disappearance of many of those marks which distinguished Catholics from other citizens. The Church has consequently become service-oriented. The sacraments are not so much a community celebration as rites dispensed to individuals who do not know one another by a priest who knows only a minority of them.

Not everything about these two models is matter for criticism. The former in particular at least had the potential for genuine community expression of joy and worship and thanksgiving. The latter undoubtedly has individuals in the congregations with the education and personal qualities to lead a mature community. But the bourgeois church has lost the joy and warmth of the earlier model, and that in its turn no longer meets the needs of adult Christians or corresponds to the social realities of the present day. Moreover, both models are deficient, the bourgeois more so than the paternalistic, in the capacity to express the unity of human life. The paternalistic church of ages gone by relativized the significance of worldly concerns and proclaimed that true happiness lay beyond this vale of tears. The bourgeois church of today is far more likely to restrict religion to a private relationship between God and the individual which is not allowed to impinge upon the conduct of life during the working week.

The mechanics of the move to the third model involve the convergence of a number of factors. The first requirement, the development of an educated Christian and Catholic laity, we already have. The second, which can also certainly be acquired, is an informed understanding of local, national, and international inequity. The third, which may in any case be coming, is personal and communal experience of social hardship and the many forms of oppression, even the most sophisticated kinds. And the fourth, which is not so easy but without which all the others will be ineffective, is that *metanoia* or change of heart which could fire us actually to do something about the practical implementation of the gospel as an expression of the love of God in Jesus Christ. This is why, if we want to find those among us who are working to build the kingdom, we may find some of them in the churches (though not all), and we may even find a few in the classrooms and the colleges of theology, but we will find them more easily among those involved in practical social movements, even those whose self-understanding does not include the idea of God or kingdom. The ecclesial models in operation will above all be those of servant and of sacrament, the latter of which suggests that the community brings the reality of the kingdom before the world, and the former that the community works for its practical implementation. Another way to say this is to say that the community exists to proclaim the gospel and to work for the kingdom, both in the local situation. Divorced either from those aims or from the local situation, it cannot perform its function, and it is no longer the Church. Let us end this section by looking a little more closely at three characteristics of the basic ecclesial community—its service, its sacramental significance, and its authority.

The believing community exists to serve the crucified in today's world. It does not exist for its own sake, therefore, but to proclaim the kingdom and to work for the realization of that kingdom here and now. It does not minister only to its own

109

members, but to the crucified, to the dispossessed, oppressed, and suffering wherever they may be—Afghan tribesmen, Brazilian Indians, Guatemalan peasants, Polish workers, and black South Africans, as well as to the poor, defenseless, and inarticulate within the parameters of the local community itself. At whatever price to itself, even to its own dissolution, it exists to give such people the freedom of the kingdom of justice and peace, a taste of heaven here and now. There are always good reasons to postpone the hour of prophecy for the sake of the preservation of the institution. If Jesus had heeded such arguments there would have been no Calvary. Consequently, it seems that at whatever price the Christian community cannot stand idly by when measures are taken in society which distance the crucified from their rightful inheritance. When political ideologies dictate courses of action which postpone the redress of genuine social inequities and intensify the structures of oppression, Christians have to oppose them, even if it means being ridiculed for political naïveté. The gospel *does* have something to say about protectionism, overseas aid, tax reform, welfare programs, education, health insurance, and so on. Politics must serve the concrete structures of human freedom, and here "freedom" does *not* mean that there must be minimum government interference in my right to trample underfoot as many other people as I wish in amassing the means to buy a Rolls-Royce or several Cadillacs, but that political activity means building the state into an organism in which all the citizens have an equal opportunity to realize fully their essential humanity.

The Church exists to serve the crucified, but it cannot simply be identified with them. Nor can all of us who claim to be the Church be correct in our claims. The Church is not the world, and is perhaps not even the Church—it is that part of the professing community which at least struggles to face squarely the sin of the world and its own implication in the structures of that sin. We are the Church when we engage in the struggle, and we are not the Church when we forget the struggle or even when we take a holiday from it. Jesus did not call us to take up our cross three days a week or forty-eight weeks a year, but daily.

A sacrament is a sign which actually participates in that which it signifies. Most of us have heard this many times before. But the political consequence of such a sacramental ecclesiology is that if the Church points to the kingdom of God's justice and peace, it is only a sacrament of that kingdom when it demonstrates the values of that kingdom, proleptically no doubt, but in reality nonetheless. It cannot proclaim justice and be an intolerant and unjust community. It cannot proclaim peace and go to war against those who do not agree with it. It cannot sow the seeds of love and joy with a face filled with hatred or suspicion. It cannot call us to a heavenly banquet if its members will allow two-thirds of the world to go to their beds hungry. It cannot be Christ's Church if it does not take the side of compassion for the suffering and oppressed to the point of its own crucifixion. Then and only then will it be a healing sacrament of the presence of God in Christ to a crucified world.

When the church fulfills its function as servant and sacrament, then it has the awful and solemn authority of Christ himself. It has a right to be heard, but that right comes only from its fidelity to its own mission. To the extent to which it is unfaithful to its mission its authority diminishes. It has no inherent right to be heard. When it is being unfaithful it is "but sounding brass and tinkling cymbal," and this faithfulness is not measured by the majesty of its words but by the quality of its praxis. This is true for the local Church, the national Church, and the universal Church. The methods of this last must be as proleptic of the values of the kingdom as the conduct of the local community. Both in the local community and the Roman Curia, political expediency can never serve the gospel.

The most difficult ecclesial problem is the assimilation in the so-called developed world of the lessons of third-world basic communities. The greatest danger, however, is that they will be dismissed as of little or no use in a radically distinct political and socio-economic climate. Doubtless, the differing societies will dictate a different order of priorities, but on the other hand we are no less in need of an ecclesial life which grows out of and addresses itself to the contemporary social situation in our countries and the world situation created in large part by the economic and political manipulation practiced by first world against third. Above all, the basic community is the mechanism for recognizing and voicing the manifold forms of oppression in the context of worship. Only in the fullness of the kingdom shall we be able to dispense with that.

Nevertheless, if we accept that it is of the essence of the Church to be rooted in the local community and its concrete problems, then some modification of the Church's instinctive self-understanding in terms of the universal Church seems to be essential. This is not to say that the Church must become less Catholic; there is no evidence that this has happened in Latin America, and indeed the opposite is true as regards traditional practice and the form of devotions. But Catholicism is part of the community's pre-understanding, that ambience in which it has grown up, even the air it breathes. The question of how that Catholicism is to be expressed in this particular situation or that is one for the local community to answer, if it is not to fall victim to a life-deadening abstraction. How this will happen in each situation will differ, though we should heed Metz's caution against identifying the basic community church with the bourgeois–liberal reaction to authority. But what seems to be of the nature of the emergence of such a Church is the conscious interweaving within a given community of prayer, worship, and reflection on the gospel on the one hand, and reflection on the inequities and oppressions of the experienced socio-political reality on the other. Basic Christian community is not something which can exist only in a Marxist society, but it does require a society not totally hypnotized by its own "freedoms," not blinded by its materialistic or capitalistic sympathies and pressure-groups. The basic Christian community can exist with ease in a free society and with difficulty in a totalitarian society; but it has no chance in a society which does not see the level of its own captivity, whether that be military, economic, psychological, or emotional.

The emergence of basic Christian communities in the West will of its nature be sporadic, since it cannot occur without some religious and political self-criticism. Some groups have existed for a long time—I am thinking of the simplicity of life of enclosed contemplative communities, or Dorothy Day's *Catholic Worker* movement in the United States—and others are more recent (such as those sectors of the Society of Jesus which have taken seriously the commitment to justice which their own highest authority demanded of them a few years ago—a commitment not totally unconnected, we should note, with the Vatican's new suspicion of the Jesuits). But these are "professional" communities. The appearance of basic communities at the parish level is of more importance for the Church as a whole. The best parishes are usually characterized by outstanding liturgical expression, genuine joy and caring, and extensive attempts at education, the "corporal works of mercy," institutional democracy, and the amelioration of local social inequalities. All these are important marks of any Christian community which dares to call itself alive. The genuine basic community *emerges* when to all the above is added a reflective dimension, a conscious connection between gospel and political structures and struggles, and a program of praxis directed toward local, national, and international objectives. All this must grow out of reflection on the gospel and analysis of the grassroots situation. The basic community will *come of age* when such a community is recognized to be the place where, first and foremost, the Church can be found.

When such a revolution in understanding takes place, it will be apparent that the credibility of the proclamation of the gospel will be in direct proportion to the clarity of its manifestation. The truth of the gospel is more evident in the lives of the community than on the pages of documents; thus, evangelization takes place most effectively when the living Christian community is made the focus of attention. And for this to happen the institutional Church must decrease in importance, or at least in visibility, to the level of a service organism for the real Church. Priests, bishops, and pope lead the community at different levels of its visibility, or they hold special roles within the educative or preaching mission. It ought to be a surprise to find them engaged in bureaucratic activity.

Concrete problems, whether for the universal, national, or local Church, ought similarly to be approached with the values of the kingdom uppermost in mind, not *a priori* principles or dead traditions. In our own situation we have particular problems and we consider various solutions to these problems; shortage of priests leads us to contemplate the pros and cons of ordaining married men, or changing the practice of the Church to take account of the desire of many women to serve in the ministry; high divorce rates are an incentive to improving the machinery of annulment or adjusting the pastoral attitude to the divorced and remarried; articulate Catholic homosexuals' groups move the Church to a more profound appreciation for sexuality; population problems and the dynamics of the family seem to lead to particular attitudes to contraception. In all these issues we respond to the problems as they exist in our culture, and with the assumptions and attitudes bred into us by living in this culture. If we add some theological sophistication, whether our own or that of our advisers, it is evident that we are in the best position to come to the right answers for our problems.

I am certainly not arguing that we have nothing to learn from others, nor that we share no common ground with others facing contemporary challenges. The entire history of the Church is a tradition of adaptation to change, and that tradition is our shared inheritance. The scriptures are another constant in our several reflections on building the kingdom in the here

114

and now, though geographical and cultural distances will affect which portions of the biblical witness speak to us most directly. Finally, we have one universal objective, wherever we are: namely, to bring forward the time of the fullness of God's kingdom by seeking to actualize its values in the here and now. Truly free people are saved people.

The common principle of pressing toward the kingdom of God is a reformulation of the central Pauline theological axiom that what is acceptable is that which "builds up the body of Christ which is the Church." It is this principle and this one alone which must dictate the wisdom of possible courses of action either in political praxis or in the revision of Church practice to make the community a more effective servant and sacrament. Consequently, such particular concerns as married or women priests, part-time clergy, lay leadership in the Church, political action, revolution, even violence, will arise as local rather than universal options, since the local or at most cultural/national context is a constant in problem-solving for the particular community, but a variable in problem-solving for the universal Church. The localization of theology has profound ecclesiological implications, and this may finally be where the enduring significance of liberation and political theology is found to reside.

NOTES

1. *Death by Bread Alone* (Philadelphia: Fortress, 1978), ch. 1.
2. *The Emergent Church* (New York: Crossroad, 1981), p. 86.

8

Political Theology
and the Vatican

IN THE YEARS SINCE Pope John Paul II assumed the helm of the bark of Peter, the role of a political theology in the universal Church has become an increasingly debated issue. With such a political pope, it was inevitable. There are, however, two quite different facets of this one concern. First, there is the matter of the character of John Paul's own "political theology," as he has demonstrated it in his speeches on many of his travels over the last six years, and especially as it emerges in his major encyclical to date, *Laborem Exercens* (1981). In the second place, Vatican (which has to mean papal) attitudes to the theology of liberation, particularly in its Latin American form, have to be considered, not only because of the way in which they depict the conflict between the historic center of the Church and its most vital current form, but also because they shed further light on what is currently deemed to be acceptable political involvement on the part of the Church.

One particular blind alley can be dismissed immediately. Current papal social teaching, and the current suspicion of the Latin American church, which the Vatican demonstrated most clearly in the 1984 document of the Congregation for the Doctrine of the Faith (CDF), *Instruction on Certain Aspects of the "Theology of Liberation,"*[1] can neither together nor separately be taken as criticism of a church which takes the side of the poor and oppressed in a struggle for justice and human rights. *Laborem Exercens'* proclamation of human work as a constitutive dimension of a dignified human life is embodied in a whole theology of economic justice. It is also widely believed that the

CDF document was, at the express wish of the pope, strengthened in its explicit statements about poverty and oppression. The preamble makes clear that, although the document has harsh words to say about some ideas of some liberation theologians,

> This warning should in no way be interpreted as a disavowal of all those who want to respond generously and with an authentic evangelical spirit to the "preferential option for the poor." It should not at all serve as an excuse for those who maintain an attitude of neutrality and indifference in the face of the tragic and pressing problems of human misery and injustice. . . . More than ever the church intends to condemn abuses, injustices, and attacks against freedom, wherever they occur and whoever commits them. She intends to struggle, by her own means, for the defense and advancement of the rights of mankind, especially of the poor.

How, then, do we balance the apparent lack of equilibrium in a papal "line" which is a strong defender of the rights of the poor but a strong critic of the "church of the poor," as the Latin American basic Christian communities have, perhaps somewhat unfortunately, come to be called? One clue lies in an article by Peter Hebblethwaite,[2] in which he argues that Catholic social teaching, that body of teaching always thought to begin with Leo XIII's *Rerum Novarum* (1891), really went out of existence with Paul VI's realization that the world had become too complex for sets of general pronouncements ever again to be useful to the universal Church, but that John Paul II is resurrecting the corpse. Paul VI, says Hebblethwaite, "did not show any contempt for [Catholic social teaching]," but "abandoned it on the grounds that it was unworkable" (91). John Paul II, on the other hand, "has deliberately set about the task of rehabilitating it" (92). Why might this be so?

The current papal style, for good or ill (and probably both), is thoroughly centrist. John Paul seems to have decided that the loss of confidence that marked the declining years of Paul VI would not mar his own tenure of office. There is much

to admire about John Paul's papacy, and some things to crit-
icize, but there is no lukewarm shilly-shallying, no lack of
clarity, no doubt about what to do next. Indeed, for some it is
the forcefulness and clarity that is precisely one of the points
about which to worry, since it seems that there might be some
matters on which clarity and the right action are not always as
easily achieved as it might seem. Great confidence and a strong
personality—perhaps we should say an utter trust in the guid-
ing presence of the Holy Spirit—are not conducive to the dele-
gation of power, nor to awareness of the possibility that some
issues are infinitely more complex than others.

As a consequence above all of the personality of the present pope, his concern to control things from the center has led
to some renewal of authoritarianism. The revivification of
Catholic social teaching, as Hebblethwaite shows so well, is one
aspect of this. It is a useful way of reasserting the role of the
Vatican as having something important to say about a whole
range of issues, whether it is the Polish or Latin American context that is envisaged, or the state of advanced capitalism. Since
Paul VI's abandonment of the notion of a universal social teaching left more responsibility with those closer to one particular
context or another, so the tightening of the reins in today's
Vatican represents an attempt to wrest back some of that local
decision-making power. This seems to meet with more resistance in Latin America than elsewhere.

It is sometimes said that John Paul II is a liberation theologian in his own right, though it perhaps makes more sense to
describe him as a specifically European political theologian.
There is no doubt that he is a believer in a real relationship between the gospel and political action, perhaps more so than any
other pope before him. As many have noted, however, there
are two restrictions which he places upon this relationship. In
the first place, it shall have nothing to do with Marxist ideology.
Second, the political implications of the gospel are the responsibility of laypeople, not of the clergy or religious, at least in

the sense of direct political involvement in some one or other public role or party platform. To this extent, the pope is an example of Gustavo Gutiérrez's "distinction of planes" model:

> The priest breaks off his point of insertion in the world. His mission is identified with that of the Church: to evangelize and to inspire the temporal order. To intervene directly in political action is to betray his function. The layman's position in the Church, on the other hand, does not require him to abandon his insertion in the world. It is his responsibility to build up both the Church and the world. In his temporal endeavors, the layman will seek to create with other men, Christian or not, a more just and more human society; he will be well aware that in so doing he is ultimately building up a society in which man will be able to respond freely to the call of God.[3]

On this view, the world and the church are very clearly separated from one another, which, like all such sophisticated dualisms, has the advantage of allowing for the autonomy of the world and of human values, but the drawback of insufficiently valuing the world from a religious perspective. To be a liberation theologian, it is necessary to be prepared to commit the whole Church, clergy and lay, to a particular option, even if that means taking sides in some concrete context. Liberation theology criticized early German political theology for its unwillingness to commit itself, for falling prey to the charms of a prophetic stance that meant keeping a critical distance from all party platforms. The Vatican of John Paul II seems to be expressing the opposite criticism of liberation theology. To be surer of this, we need to take a closer look at the CDF Declaration.

The document, identified more with the Prefect of the Congregation, Cardinal Ratzinger, than with the pope, defends the aspiration to liberation as "the authentic, if obscure, perception of the dignity of the human person" (I), but suggests that such yearning needs "to be clarified and guided," since it "often finds itself the captive of ideologies which hide or pervert its meaning" (II). Liberation is, of course, a Christian theme, but the doctrinal frontiers between acceptable and unacceptable understandings of the "theology of liberation" are "badly defined" (III). The scriptures certainly support a theology of liberation, though one that subordinates social sin to personal sin (IV). Moreover, the social teaching of the Church, at least since John XXIII, has reinforced this attention to the poor and oppressed (V).

With these preambles, the text of the Declaration is ready to make its major points. In section VI, "A New Interpretation of Christianity," the CDF makes clear its intention to deal only with the pathological variations on liberation theology, which propose "a novel interpretation of both the content of faith and of Christian existence which seriously departs from the faith of the church and, in fact, actually constitutes a practical negation." The twin attendant evils are declared to be "concepts uncritically borrowed from Marxist ideology and recourse to theses of a biblical hermeneutic marked by rationalism." The criticisms of the document since it has appeared have focused on the question whether such pathological variants in fact exist anywhere other than in the minds of the members of the CDF.

On Marxism, the Declaration argues that analysis and ideology cannot be separated, that notions like that of class conflict cannot be isolated from the ideology which gave birth to them, and that atheism is at the heart of Marxism. The use of analytical methods like Marxism, says the CDF, is instrumental and "must undergo a critical study from a theological perspective." Clearly, there is room for conflict here, since liberation theology will want to argue that any theological perspective is itself likely to have a particular ideological slant, while the CDF is obviously of the opinion that there is something called "theology" which exists in a social, political, and probably historical vacuum. When the CDF goes on to argue that "the first condition for any analysis is total openness to the reality to be described," and to warn of the dangers of ideological bias, it is clearly oblivious of the dangers of its own false consciousness.

Section VIII of the CDF document gets to the heart of the problem. The ideological core borrowed from Marxism, it says, leads to a belief that it is only through the class struggle that truth is achieved, and therefore that truth is attached to "partisan praxis" which will involve violent struggle. In the writings of certain (unnamed) theologians of liberation, this leads to a belief that the class struggle divides the Church itself, and that that profane history which is indistinguishable from salvation history is in fact nothing other than "the process of the self-redemption of man by means of the class struggle." Faith, hope, and charity are "emptied of their theological reality" by being defined as "fidelity to history," "confidence in the future," and "option for the poor." The church itself is made a secular reality, the church of the poor is identified with the proletariat of Marx, the hierarchy with the oppressor class, Catholic social teaching is "reformist compromise," liberation theologians engage in a "reductionist reading of the Bible," and are open to immanentism and rationalism.

Rarely can there have been such a devastatingly comprehensive criticism directed at an invisible group of people. Nowhere are names named or even hinted at, nowhere are the perpetrators of these arguments quoted. Subsequent events have confirmed the suspicion that Gustavo Gutiérrez and Leonardo Boff were at least among those the CDF had in mind, since both were investigated in Rome at some length. Gutiérrez seems to have escaped for the moment, perhaps because of the surprising amount of support for him from a moderately conservative Peruvian hierarchy. Boff has been "silenced" for a while, despite the intervention on his behalf of senior Brazilian bishops, but, given the polemical tone of parts of his recent *Church: Charism and Power*,[4] that is hardly surprising. The Vatican is unlikely to look in a kindly fashion on someone who submits the structure of the Church itself to Marxist analysis, even if on the whole the accompanying ecclesiology is unexceptionable.

Leaving aside the tricky question of just how much accuracy the Vatican critique possesses, either as an attack on Boff and Gutiérrez or on other liberation theologians, a number of more general charges are at least worth discussing. They cluster around two general observations: first, that liberation theology is reducing theology to a secular matter; second, that its view of the world is too heavily influenced by Marxism. We shall have to examine some of the more specific criticisms made under each of these headings.

Liberation theology has developed a notion of "structural sin," which refers to sin as witting or vincibly ignorant involvement in objectively oppressive social structures. The Vatican suspects that this notion represents a politization of the idea of sin, removing the more traditional idea of sin as a personal act offending God and/or my neighbor. However, this seems not to take account of the classical Christian notion of the "sin of omission." Structural sin is one kind of sin of omission, sin above all by indifference to the injustice in my society that I can indeed at least strive to do something about.

There is no justification for representing the reduction of the idea of sin to that of social sin as characteristic even of *some* liberation theologians. The Latin American Bishops Conference at Medellín, Colombia, in 1968 clearly stated the priority of personal conversion over political struggle:

> The uniqueness of the Christian message does not so much consist in the affirmation of the necessity for structural change, as it does in the insistence on the conversion of men which will in turn bring about this change. We will not have a new continent without new and reformed structures, but, above all, there will be no new continent without new men, who know how to be truly free and responsible according to the light of the gospel.

Moreover, even Boff, whom the CDF has in mind (if it has anyone in mind at all), points out in his recent book on the Church that a major limitation of liberation theology is that "it runs the risk of ignoring the need for personal conversion" (p. 21).

A second aspect of the theological critique focuses on the suspicion that liberation theology is engaged in creating a "local theology," which would suggest that there is no such thing as the universal truth of faith, upon which belief all traditional theological teaching in fact depends. Of course, even the central teaching "magisterium" of the Church has become aware that it must learn to formulate what has to be said in ways appropriate to the backgrounds of those it is addressing. In Roman Catholicism in recent decades this missiological imperative has most usually been referred to as "inculturation." The gospel had to be inculturated into the cultural context of the mission. Liberation theology resists such language, since it sounds like something fundamentally European (and therefore the product of the historical oppressor), which is going to be re-presented in some more digestible local variation. This is not sufficient. On the contrary, the gospel must be heard afresh from a standpoint within the culture, and a local theology will emerge as the historic and culturally conditioned experience of the community leads the people to hear the gospel in a new way.

The Vatican's suspicion is of course that such theologies will be beyond its control, beyond approbation or censure. Hence the CDF describes the role of the theologians as one in which they will "collaborate loyally and with a spirit of dialogue with the magisterium of the church. They will be able to recognize in the magisterium a gift of Christ to his church and will welcome its word and its directives with filial respect." Theologians may perhaps be forgiven for thinking that this is not quite dialogue. More importantly, the issue for them is not one of control or lack of it, but of the only conditions under which theology can be done. There is no such thing as an uncontextual theology. Theology originating in the Vatican is just as contextual, just as open to historical and cultural influences,

124

as any other. But the CDF persists in the belief that there is such a thing as a purely theological judgment which can escape historical conditioning.

This leads neatly to the third and perhaps most serious charge, that liberation theology collapses secular and salvation history into one reality. The term that the CDF uses is "historicist immanentism," which seems to mean that salvation is reduced to the utopia that comes at the end of the earthly struggle against oppression. This, however, is not what liberation theologians say. In an article entitled "Capitalism and Socialism: A Theological Crux,"[5] Juan Luis Segundo compares two approaches to the relationship between religion and politics. In the first, matters to do with the individual's relationship to God are given absolute significance, and matters of "historical functionality" are relativized. That is to say, the really important thing in life is a direct approach to salvation through membership in the Church, prayer, sacraments, and so on, and the social and political are as important as they are helpful in making this possible. The second view is that human life in society has absolute value, and that religious institutions, dogmas, and so on are only instrumental or functional to this absolute.

There are, in fact, two understandings at work of how salvation is achieved: the former sees it in a flight from the world into the things of religion; the latter, in the struggle for authentic humanity in which the things of religion can help. God gives the kingdom in God's good time: the Christian community's approach to the kingdom is through the struggle here and now to live by the values of the kingdom which can only be in its fullness at the end of time. Historical involvement is therefore the best preparation for God's kingdom. This view is of course quite opposed to a true "historicist immanentism," which would deny the other-worldly reality of the kingdom of God. Liberation theology simply argues that the closest human beings can come to that kingdom in history is not to flee the world, but to struggle for justice in the world.

125

When we turn to the criticisms of too much use of or involvement with Marxist analysis and/or ideology, the charges focus upon the notion of class consciousness. Liberation theologians, at least some of them, says the CDF, have come to equate truth with praxis. That is, they have identified involvement in the revolutionary struggle of the poor as the privileged locus from which "reality" can be correctly perceived. From this emerges their arrogance about all other ways of doing theology, which are not true insofar as they do not grow out of praxis. Moreover, this struggle of the poor, this class-warfare notion, becomes *the* interpretation of history. Historical progress, hence liberation and even salvation, stems from involvement in the class struggle. So to represent the Christian message is to make central to the gospel the notion of conflict between peoples, whereas the heart of the gospel is a message of love and reconciliation. It is to have recourse to violence in the name of peace. In general, it exhibits the mistaken assumption that ideas can be borrowed from Marxist analysis piecemeal, whereas the truth is that to use the terminology of Marxism is to play with fire, and to put dangerous notions into the heads of well-meaning people without the critical understanding to evaluate them.

There is no doubt that liberation theologians use terminology drawn from the thought of Marx. So do most Latin American intellectuals and most European intellectuals, many North Americans, and even the pope himself, whose *Laborem Exercens* is redolent of Marx's analysis of the alienating effects of capitalism. The issue is whether they use these ideas freely, that is, without becoming dupes of the logic of a Marxism that is perceived as ending in totalitarianism and atheism. As Arthur McGovern, s.j. has suggested in a very helpful article,[6] attention to the historical development of Marxism reveals that it has taken and continues to take many forms, and that current Marxist–Leninist Soviet-style government is neither the only

126

possible form nor the one that has most influence in Latin America, though it is certainly the form best known to the present pope with his experience of life in a Soviet satellite.

In the case of the particular notion of class struggle, liberation theologians will themselves say that they are not even adopting the Marxist ideological position that class struggle must take place, but simply recognizing that as a matter of fact in most Latin American societies there is class division, class warfare, and progress seems to be possible only through the identification of the church with the majority underclass. Moreover, they will argue that they are not advocating violence (again, Medellín was very clear about that), and that conflict is not the heart of the gospel, but that the one message of the gospel may, precisely because it singles out the poor as God's special concern, mean peace to some and cause conflict for others.

The real heart of the conflict between the Vatican and liberation theologians may be more apparent in the condemnation of Leonardo Boff. In his most recent book, as we mentioned above, Boff presents a criticism of the hierarchical, institutional model of the Church, preferring to that a "people of God" model that he finds expressed in the Latin American basic Christian community. In a Marxist analysis, he accuses the clergy of expropriating the means of "religious production" to themselves, at the expense of the laity. He has many harsh things to say about abuses of power. He claims the right to speak as a prophet.

Once again, it is Cardinal Ratzinger's CDF which has the duty of replying on behalf of the Holy See. Many of its comments echo the language of the Declaration, as for example when it argues that "praxis neither replaces nor produces the truth, but remains at the service of the truth consigned to us by the Lord." More clearly than in the Declaration, however, this "notification"[7] shows that the real issue is one of control. Not only is the theologian obliged to a contextual rendering of a non-contextual truth enunciated by the magisterium, but even prophecy is said to be controlled by the church:

> In order to be legitimate, prophetic denunciation in the church must always remain at the service of the church itself. Not only must it accept the hierarchy and the institutions, but it must also cooperate positively in the consolidation of the church's internal communion; furthermore, the supreme criterion for judging not only its ordinary exercise but also its genuineness pertains to the hierarchy.[8]

One might be forgiven for wondering how much genuine prophecy would survive the test of hierarchical approval, or what would have been the fate of the words of Jeremiah or Amos or Hosea if they had come before the CDF.

There have always, from the very earliest years of the Christian community, been tensions evident between warring human impulses. On the one hand, the human desire to organize, to systematize, and to legalize the community led within the space of a century to the beginnings of Catholicism, understood not so much as the Roman Catholic Church of today, though that is its descendant, but as the belief in the visible institution as the sacrament of salvation. On the other hand, the urge to throw off the shackles of that institutionalization in order to be freer to express the vitality of the gospel was evident equally early in the Pauline communities. The necessities of an historical community led to the preponderance of the former impulse, and the latter was consigned by slow degrees to heresies and to Protestantism.

The current conflict is an example of the old tension, reaching into the twentieth century within the Catholic Church. In this case as in so many others before it, the options are the same: either dialogue and understanding, or anathemas and over-statement of differences, leading, if not to schism, at least to bitterness and defections. The CDF talks in both documents about the role of the theologian in reading the signs of the times, evaluating contemporary history theologically. The CDF is itself bound to the same process, and that means recognizing that Europeanization, colonialism, bad historical sense, and lust for power have all played their part in the domination of the Church by the Roman establishment. The Latin American church, on the other hand, has to recognize that the presence of demonic elements in the bureaucratic practice of the Church does not amount to a demonic institution, still less an evil and power-hungry hierarchy.

The current controversy cannot, however, be dealt with solely on such a both/and basis. It seems clear to me that there is an imbalance here, and that it is that the Vatican is really more suspicious of liberation theology than it has a need or even a right to be. Part of the problem stems, as we said above, from the current pope's determination to keep a short rein on the Church. Much more of it has to do with a one-sided set of advisers on Latin America (the English Jesuit journal, *The Month*, recently suggested that some of them might be in the pay of the CIA!). Still more is caused by giving Cardinal Ratzinger's over-zealous CDF too free a hand. The traditional Eurocentric racism of the Roman Church has something to do with it too (for example, the first Latin American cardinal was named in 1905, over 400 years after the arrival of Catholicism in that continent, and after the United States, Canada, and even Australia had had a red hat or two to their names). Above all, however, it stems from clerical forgetfulness of the origins of the church, and the true power at work in it. The attitude of the institutional Church to liberation theology at the present time can be illustrated by the story of a former acquaintance of mine, a Jesuit priest, who came home one day full of indignation. He had been preaching a sermon and someone had stood up in the congregation in the middle of his sermon and cried, "Praise the Lord!" Pointing a sternly rebuking finger at the person, the priest shouted, "Sit down! I will tell you when to say 'Praise the Lord'!" The institutional Church, like my friend, is in danger of forgetting that the voice of the Spirit can never be silenced. It blows when it will, where it will, and just as much as it will.

NOTES

1. *Origins,* NC Documentary Service, 14 No. 13 (13 September 1984), 193–204.

2. "The Popes and Politics: Shifting Patterns in 'Catholic Social Doctrine'," *Daedalus* 111 (Winter 1982), 85–98.

3. *A Theology of Liberation,* p. 57.

4. (New York: Crossroad, 1985).

5. In *Liberation South, Liberation North,* ed. Michael Novak (Washington: American Enterprise Institute, 1981), pp. 7–23.

6. "Should a Christian Be a Marxist?" in *Ethical Wisdom East and/ or West* (=*Proceedings* of the American Catholic Philosophical Association 51 [1977]), pp. 220–30.

7. *Origins* 14 No. 42 (4 April 1985), 683–87.

8. Ibid., 687.

Whence Political Theology?

THROUGHOUT THIS BOOK, the term "political theology" has been used without apology or preface, and frequently interchangeably with the related term "liberation theology." True, an attempt has been made to explain and describe the phenomenon to which it refers, but not to uncover the origins of the term itself. In fact, the phrase has been used in different ways for many centuries, and it seems appropriate to say something about the origin of the current usage, and of its relationship to the so-called theology of liberation. In the course of this brief explanation, it will also be possible to make some suggestions for further reading at greater depth than this present introductory study.

Some readers may have imagined that the term "political theology" is a new coinage, as the reality to which it refers here is certainly a new phenomenon in the Christian churches. Others who are perhaps more theologically literate may think it is one of the classical divisions of the theological enterprise, and those even better versed in the history of ideas may know of previous "political theologies" and reasonably conclude that the present object of study is related to some or all of them. In fact, all of these assumptions, reasonable enough in themselves, would be erroneous.

In this book, "political theology" refers to a reality which relates, if it does not fuse together, two distinct theological developments. For this reason, if for no other, it has little to do with the earlier usage of the term, and I propose to say no more about earlier forms of political theology. The interested reader may wish to consult Johann Baptist Metz's article under the heading "Political Theology" in *Sacramentum Mundi*,[1] or the much fuller and really indispensable treatment of the historical development of political theology to be found in Francis Schussler Fiorenza's article, "Political Theology as Foundational Theology," *Proceedings* of the Catholic Theological Society of America 32 (1977), 142–77.

The first of the two contemporary theological trends treated here under the rubric of political theology is the one known, rather confusingly, as "political theology." This geographically circumscribed movement centers in the work of three German theologians, Johann Baptist Metz, Jürgen Moltmann, and Dorothee Soelle, who have developed their particular perspectives in response to the Enlightenment and in dialogue with the critical social theorists of the Frankfurt school. Of the three, Metz is perhaps the most easily identified with political theology, and for that reason the one in the forefront of the minds of liberation theologians when criticizing European political theology for its abstractness and lack of concrete political commitment. The essential works of Metz are three: to begin with his *Theology of the World* (New York: Herder, 1971) is to see immediately what the liberation theologians found suspect; to read on in *Faith in History and Society* (New York: Seabury, 1980) is to see Metz accepting the justice of some of those criticisms and modifying his position accordingly; to consult *The Emergent Church* (New York: Crossroad, 1981) is to find him explicitly recognizing that in many ways the church of the so-called third world has become the teacher, and that the first-world, European church now finds itself in the unaccustomed position of pupil. Both Moltmann and Soelle complement Metz in different ways, the former placing his interest in political theology in the context of a classically conceived and executed theological body of work,[2] the latter abandoning an earlier systematic approach for a more journalistic style and a more direct address of contemporary issues.[3] Among recent studies of political theology in this narrower sense of the term are Charles Davis' work on the role of critical social theory in political theology, *Theology and Political Society* (Cambridge: Cambridge University Press, 1980), and the much more accessible study by John Cobb, *Process Theology as Political Theology* (Philadelphia: Westminster, 1982).

The world of German political theology is the secularized, commercialized, materialistic, behavioral, and alienated world of middle and late twentieth century. Political theology in its more European, more theoretical dress is best explained, it seems, as a responsible Christian addressing of that secularized world. Dietrich

Bonhoeffer's characterization of our world as "come of age" points to the unquestionable autonomy of the secular, and the right and responsibility of the secular citizen to engage in the everyday world without having to provide some supernatural justification. The church which wants to take this world seriously and yet to remain the church has to see human involvement in the full complexity of that world as integral to salvation. The *saeculum* can no longer be either allegorized or dismissed; it has to be taken seriously on its own terms. If the church turns its back on the world, or tries to pretend that nothing is changed since the Middle Ages, the chances are that its unpreparedness to meet the needs and crises of this world will be matched by its loss of credibility. Ironically, Bonhoeffer's dictum was coined in a prison cell which might never have existed if Christians in Europe had taken sufficiently seriously their responsibility to the world "come of age." Entirely appropriately, it was from Germany, with its need to purge the memory of Nazism, with its present-day tax-supported institutional and bourgeois religion, that the new political theology emerged.

The history of the development of liberation theology is more central to our concern. The origins of this movement do not lie in the West, but are in some sense a response to the impact of the West on the third world. If political theology in the narrow sense is a reaction to the internal conditions of the first world, then liberation theology began as a reaction to the colonial legacy of the first world to the third. Latin America, place of origin of liberation theology, has existed under one or other form of colonial influence for the whole of the last five hundred years. The rule of Spain and Portugal was replaced by the no-less-pervasive economic domination of first England and then the United States. That relationship still exists today, and explains in large part most if not all the ills which beset the continent, from the deep socio-economic divisions, to extreme financial dependence, to violent liberation struggles, to the role of Marxist and socialist pressure-groups. An excellent history of Latin America told from the perspective of liberation theology is Enrique Dussel's *A History of the Church in Latin America: From Colonialism to Liberation* (Grand Rapids: Eerdmans, 1981). Dussel, a leading Latin American Protestant theologian, has produced a hermeneu-

133

tically sophisticated study of the development from colonial to liberation church.

Liberation theology originated as the response of the church and church people to the political and socio-economic malaise of Latin America. However, the fact that such a response occurred at this time rather than at some other requires explanation, and this must partially be sought in the general revolution in attitudes within the Catholic Church since the beginning of this century. The three areas in which this radical shift has had most effect upon theology, and hence upon liberation theology, are in the scientific study of the scriptures, in the openness to the investigations of the social sciences, and in the developing tradition of the "social teaching" of the Church. I can make no attempt here to provide even a basic bibliography for the theological revolution of the twentieth century, but three representative works which show how liberation theology has benefited from each of these three areas are José Miranda's *Marx and the Bible* (Maryknoll: Orbis, 1974), Juan Luis Segundo's *The Liberation of Theology* (Maryknoll: Orbis, 1976), and Donal Dorr's *Option for the Poor* (Maryknoll: Orbis, 1984).

Explaining the changes that came about in the Catholic Church in mid-century is no easy task. For all his autocratic spirit, it is probably to Pius XII that credit must go for beginning the long, slow thaw after the ice age of Pius X. Pius XII encouraged the scientific study of the Bible and eased the anti-modernist atmosphere which had gripped the Church for half a century, bedeviling theological research. It is worth remembering that most of the liberation theologians, at least of the first generation, were trained in seminaries and universities organized on preconciliar lines, and credit for some of their intellectual flexibility should go to that same church.

It is certainly correct, however, to see the major shift in the Church's attitudes symbolized in the ample figure of John XXIII, whose expressed desire to throw open the windows and let in a little air led to the Second Vatican Council, and hence to the Church as we know it today, with its mixture of preconciliar foot-dragging, conciliar enthusiasm, and postconciliar strife.[4] In the two major encyclicals of his brief reign, *Mater et Magistra* (1961) and *Pacem in Terris* (1963), the social teaching acquired a new tone, a new sense of participation and solidarity with other groups seeking justice on earth. That same spirit of cooperation is also evident in the council's *Pastoral Constitution on the Church in the Modern World*, and perhaps above all in Paul VI's *Populorum Progressio*, surely the greatest social document yet produced by a pope. There are two useful collections of documents of Catholic social teaching. Joseph Gremillion's *The Gospel of Peace and Justice* (Maryknoll: Orbis, 1976) has the advantage of a lengthy and excellent introduction, and includes the major documents of the popes from John XXIII to Paul VI's 1975 address for World Peace Day, as well as three of the documents of the immensely important 1968 Medellín conference of the Latin American Bishops. The more recent compilation by Michael Walsh and Brian Davies, *Proclaiming Justice and Peace* (Mystic: Twenty-Third Publications, 1985), restricts itself to papal encyclicals, and has a much briefer introduction, but of course includes the present pope's three major letters, two of which are significant in establishing the complex attitudes of the current Vatican administration to political and liberation theologies.

Although over the last twenty-five years papal encyclicals have paid increasing attention to the problems of the so-called third world, it would be a mistake to think of liberation theology as simply growing out of an application of the social teaching of the Church to a specific geographic area. In fact, papal attention to issues of development and human rights is as much a response to movements in third-world churches as it is a stimulus to their awareness. The Medellín conference itself, though sometimes interpreted as a Latin American application of the Vatican Council teaching, gave official approbation to movements in the Church of that continent that went far beyond the essentially liberal and reformist approach of the Council. Liberation theology has to be explained far more as an indigenous development in response to peculiarly regional problems than as a branch of world-wide *aggiornamento*.

The period of the late sixties and early seventies was that of the great ferment of Latin American liberation theology, and also that in which it was most misunderstood, admittedly sometimes as a result of the excesses of its adherents. Too often it was assumed to be a theology of revolution, with Camilo Torres, the Colombian "guerilla priest," as its typical exponent. Torres' writings have been collected and published in English translation.[5] A far better example of the essential charisms of liberation theology from that earlier period would be the figure of Dom Helder Camara, archbishop of Recife in northeastern Brazil,[6] and from more recent times that of the martyred archbishop of San Salvador, Oscar Romero.[7] In very similar ways the two demonstrated that compassion, solidarity, and non-violence are the true heart of the theology of liberation.

The actual bibliography of liberation theology is now quite beyond any one individual's control, but an attempt must be made to point to at least some of the major works beyond those already mentioned. Even more than fifteen years on, liberation theology cannot be appreciated without reading Gustavo Gutiérrez's classic *A Theology of Liberation* (Maryknoll: Orbis, 1973). However, the distance that the movement has come can clearly be seen in the more recent writings of Gutiérrez, *The Power of the Poor in History* (Maryknoll: Orbis, 1983) and *We Drink from Our Own Wells* (Maryknoll: Orbis, 1984). In these works there is far less theology in the normal sense of the word, and far more response to the voiced experience of the poor of Latin America themselves. This reflection upon the experience of oppression is the first step in the liberation process. As Gutiérrez himself has said, "theology comes after." The reflection itself takes place not in academic circles but in the Basic Christian Communities which have mushroomed in many Latin American countries. In fact, some appreciation of these BCCs is essential to a correct perception of the phenomenon of liberation theology as a popular, grassroots movement. There are a number of valuable works, among them Alvaro Barreiro's *Basic Communities: The Evangelization of the Poor* (Maryknoll: Orbis, 1982) and a collection of papers edited by John Eagleson and Sergio Torres, *The Challenge of Basic Christian Communities* (Maryknoll: Orbis, 1981). In addition there are good, more popular discussions of what these communities are actually like in Richard Shaull's *Heralds of a New Reformation: The Poor of South and North America* (Maryknoll: Orbis, 1984) and especially in Harvey Cox's recent *Religion in the Secular City.*[8]

Works on Latin American liberation theology divide into those written by Latin Americans themselves and those written by others (mostly North Americans) to explain the phenomenon or to consider its potential applicability in the first world. Among the more significant publications from Orbis Books (which anyone who has turned to the notes must rapidly have realized is the dominant publisher in this field) in the first category are the three works by Gustavo Gutiérrez and the one by José Miranda already mentioned, Jon Sobrino's *Christology at the Crossroads* (1978), Leonardo Boff's *Jesus Christ Liberator* (1978) and *Liberating Grace* (1981), Hugo Assmann's *Theology for a Nomad Church* (1975), and Pierre Bigo's *The Church and Third World Revolution* (1977). From other publishers there are José Miguez Bonino's *Towards a Christian Political Ethics* (Philadelphia: Fortress, 1983), and the rather elderly but still valuable work by Rubem Alves, *A Theology of Human Hope* (St. Meinrad: Abbey Press, 1969).

Books that discuss the theology of liberation from a first-world perspective have mushroomed more recently, as more and more people become aware of what it has to offer, and as the lack of confidence of the early stages of its appropriation wanes. Once again, Orbis leads the field in number and overall quality of books. Among the best of those not so far mentioned are Philip Berryman's *The Religious Roots of Rebellion: Christians in Central American Revolutions* (1984), Adam Daniel Finnerty's *No More Plastic Jesus: Global Justice and the Christian Lifestyle* (1977), and Alfred Hennelly's *Theologies in Conflict: The Challenge of Juan Luis Segundo* (1979). A critical but perceptive study of liberation theology, comparing it with the thought of Reinhold Niebuhr, is Dennis McCann's *Christian Realism and Liberation Theology* (Maryknoll: Orbis, 1981). From other publishers, two works stand out: Robert McAfee Brown's *Theology in a New Key* (Philadelphia: Westminster, 1978) and Schubert Ogden's *Faith and Freedom* (Nashville: Abingdon Press, 1979).

The last category of works that should be mentioned demonstrates something of the flowering of liberation theology in groups beyond Latin America which, like the Latin Americans, struggle for solidarity against perceived structural oppression. First among these, at least chronologically, one would have to name black American theology of liberation, and here James Cone's two major works remain seminal. They are *A Black Theology of Liberation* (Philadelphia: Lippincott, 1970), and *God of the Oppressed* (New York: Seabury, 1975). The most developed area is, however, feminist thought, and here the most interesting figures are both American, Rosemary Radford Ruether and Elizabeth Schussler Fiorenza. The former appeared on the scene earlier, with works like *Liberation Theology: Human Hope Confronts Christian History and American Power* (New York: Paulist, 1972), *New Woman, New Earth: Sexist Ideologies and Human Liberation* (New York: Seabury, 1975), and *Religion and Sexism: Images of Women in Jewish and Christian Tradition* (New York: Simon & Schuster, 1974). Fiorenza's most recent work, *In Memory of Her* (New York: Crossroad, 1983), may well be the most substantial feminist theology to date. Finally, there are the theologies emerging from other parts of the "developing" world that owe something to Latin American liberation theology. A good collection of representative writings, edited by John C. England, is *Living Theology in Asia* (Maryknoll: Orbis, 1982), while Tissa Balasuriya's *The Eucharist and Human Liberation* (Maryknoll: Orbis, 1980) and *Planetary Theology* (Maryknoll: Orbis, 1984) are interesting works from the perspective of a Christian in Buddhist Sri Lanka. In African thought, in which writings are not yet so extensive, there are two works from white theologians, Aylward Shorter's *African Christian Theology: Adaptation or Incarnation* (Maryknoll: Orbis, 1977) and Albert Nolan's *Jesus Before Christianity: The Gospel of Liberation* (London: Darton, Longman and Todd, 1977). A number of essays focusing on the African dimension of liberation theology are to be found in volumes reprinting papers from the Ecumenical Dialogue of Third World Theologians. Two volumes in particular stand out, both edited by Virginia Fabella and Sergio Torres: seven papers are collected in *The Emergent Gospel: Theology from the Underside of History* (Maryknoll: Orbis, 1976), and there is one interesting essay by Bonganjalo Goba in *Irruption of the Third World* (Maryknoll: Orbis, 1983). There is no doubt that there will be many more.

NOTES

1. *Sacramentum Mundi: An Encyclopedia of Theology*, edd. K. Rahner and H. Vorgrimler (London: Burns & Oates, 1970).

2. Moltmann's great theological trilogy is well known. It began with *Theology of Hope* (New York: Harper & Row, 1967), continued with *The Crucified God* (New York: Harper & Row, 1974), and was brought to a conclusion with *The Church in the Power of the Spirit* (New York: Harper & Row, 1977). A series of shorter works deals more explicitly with political theology, principal among them being *Religion, Revolution and the Future* (New York: Scribners, 1969), *The Experiment Hope* (Philadelphia: Fortress, 1975), *The Power of the Powerless* (New York: Harper & Row, 1983), and *On Human Dignity: Political Theology and Ethics* (Philadelphia: Fortress, 1984).

3. The best introduction to Soelle's thought is her own *Political Theology* (Philadelphia: Fortress, 1984).

4. A useful and entertaining history of the Catholic Church since the Second Vatican Council is Peter Hebblewaite, *The Runaway Church* (New York: Seabury, 1975).

5. *Camilo Torres: Revolutionary Writings* (New York: Herder, 1969). In English there is also *Revolutionary Priest: The Complete Writings and Messages of Camilo Torres*, ed. John Gerassi (New York: Vintage, 1971).

6. See his own *The Desert Is Fertile* (Maryknoll: Orbis, 1981) and *Hoping Against Hope* (Maryknoll: Orbis, 1984).

7. See James R. Brockman, *The Word Remains: A Life of Oscar Romero* (Maryknoll: Orbis, 1982).

8. (New York: Simon & Schuster, 1984), pp. 98–158.